ESSENTIALS
OF LIBERAL EDUCATION

BY

D. LUTHER EVANS

JUNIOR DEAN AND PROFESSOR OF PHILOSOPHY

COLLEGE OF ARTS AND SCIENCES

THE OHIO STATE UNIVERSITY

19,206

GINN AND COMPANY

BOSTON · NEW YORK · CHICAGO · ATLANTA · DALLAS · COLUMBUS
SAN FRANCISCO · TORONTO · LONDON

6 – 10 – 42

The Athenæum Press

GINN AND COMPANY · PRO-
PRIETORS · BOSTON · U.S.A.

FOREWORD

THIS BOOK is designed for college students and other persons who may wish to examine thoughtfully the fundamentals of a liberal education. To state the purpose of the book in another way, I have tried to show how important the cultural college is in contemporary American life. No effort is made to evaluate the activities of vocational and professional schools, but the assumption that a general, liberal education is prerequisite to effective specialized training is frankly accepted. The work is not intended to be a practical guidebook for bewildered freshmen. I do not pretend to tell all the things which the successful college student ought to know. Very little advice is offered regarding social adjustments, care of health, financial problems, or choice of a vocation. The emphasis is upon the more fundamental aspects of the campus experience, — the cultural and curricular aspects, — and these are interpreted in the light of a total life outlook. A definite attempt is made to show the student *why*, *how*, and *what* he ought to study in college, but these specific objectives are related directly to the development of a broad and vital philosophy of human living. The book, in short, aims to be an informal and elementary introduction to liberal education. Although the chapters were planned with the college undergraduate especially in mind, answers are suggested to many questions frequently raised by parents, professors, and educational advisers. Most of the discussions will be of pointed interest to high-school seniors who wish information concerning the ideals and activities of the cultural college.

With all Americans, young and old, who believe that liberal education can bring to the people of a nation the sympathy and understanding necessary for free and creative social living, I join in a common affirmation of faith. If somewhere in the following pages the reader is persuaded that the American college can provide the basic knowledge and the moral vision upon which the cultural and political future of our country must depend, the dominant purpose of this work will have been realized. The underlying thesis is the belief that what distressed and chaotic society needs more than anything else is the guidance of individuals who, through fundamental and comprehensive thought, can solve the momentous problems of our tragic age. In an era of terror and violence, of hatred and fear, we must look to the interpreters of liberal culture for the rational insight without which civilization will lose its meaning and its purpose.

This is no plea for vague, utopian, wishful thinking in our social responses. The liberal education which will lead humanity out of chaos into order must be grounded in critically examined and logically organized factual knowledge. Sound and workable knowledge must not only interpret objectives of human activity; it must include also an adequate understanding of the methods and means by which these objectives may be realized.

iv

The concept of culture which I seek to defend is no grandiose, superhuman idea-force. The liberal ideal opposes the totalitarian and absolutistic theory of culture. Culture is not a huge national social force expressing the will of an autocratic superstate. Culture, in the democratic tradition, has its residence in the minds and hearts of individual men and women. It is not impressed on private minds by dictatorial indoctrinating powers. The cultural privileges of liberal education are the attainment of free, aspiring, and responsible human beings, who know the purposes, principles, and procedures of effective individual and social living. No college perspective can be valid or valuable which ignores, in its total view, the exigencies and needs of everyday experience.

In the attempt to present an idealistic educational outlook which realistically recognizes the actual problems of contemporary human existence the book examines four great issues. In the first place, it seeks to show that the notion of rational and responsible personality is a major and persistent ideal of the whole cultural tradition. In the second place, the techniques of learning which are most effective both in academic and in professional activity are fully described. In the third place, the contents and functions of the various college curricula are examined, and the importance of the different courses of study for individual and communal life is indicated. Finally, the values of liberal education in the democratic process are discussed, and the duties of the educated person to the social order are outlined. The book is a defense and analysis of four great attainments of man: *The Art of Self-Discovery*, *The Art of Self-Discipline*, *The Art of Self-Development*, and *The Art of Self-Denial*. United in one all-inclusive response, these four arts constitute, I suggest, the greatest of all human achievements — *The Art of Living*.

The following pages reflect mainly the experiences which, as a personnel dean and professor, I have been privileged to enjoy at the College of Wooster and The Ohio State University. The book also reflects many happy associations on the faculties of Ohio Wesleyan University and The University of Wisconsin. From Dean Bland L. Stradley and the Administrative Staff of the College of Arts and Sciences of The Ohio State University and from my colleagues in the Department of Philosophy I have received very helpful ideas in the areas of college procedure and theory. My fellowship with the Junior Deans of The Ohio State University has been a continuous source of enjoyment and profit. I have also found very stimulating the educational views of Dean Walter S. Gamertsfelder of Ohio University. The editors of *Education* have kindly permitted me to use some excerpts from articles which I have published in their journal.

Acknowledged with special appreciation is the valuable help which, in the preparation of part III, I received from Mr. Alvin F. Nelson and Miss Sarah M. Watson, graduate assistants in the Department of Philosophy of The Ohio State University.

D.L.E.

CONTENTS

vii

ESSENTIALS
OF LIBERAL EDUCATION

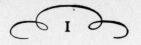

THE ART
OF SELF-DISCOVERY

IDEALS
OF LIBERAL EDUCATION

NO INSTITUTION which does not advance the welfare of humanity is worthy of support or survival. Useless organizations are as deplorable as useless individuals. Colleges cannot be exempt from this requirement. If liberal education does not convincingly promote the well-being of men and women, it cannot justly command their approval and loyalty. The problems and difficulties now facing mankind are too momentous to permit the continuance of wasteful and futile social institutions. When the whole structure of society is being shaken, colleges must be very clear and sound in their pronouncements.

1. *The Call of the College*

In this book I seek to show that the college of liberal arts plays a tremendously important role in the advancement of humanity. Our nation and all nations need desperately today the intellectual and moral virtues which the cultural colleges eminently promote. Defining character as integrated, rational, and altruistic personality, I contend that the development of character is the supreme task and privilege of the college of today. The future of civilization will depend upon human beings who know social righteousness as well as scientific truth. Enlightenment without ethics is a social menace and an educational fraud.

The progress of the race can be assured only if the liberal college, as a persistent defender of spiritual values, remains powerful and free. If, in this brutalized age, America is to lead in the conquest of violence and terror, her college graduates will have to be men and women of loyalty, courage, and faith. Educators may differ today in their views about the essentials of human living, but, more and more, they are agreed that higher learning must be concerned with the fundamental moral and social principles upon which a creative and harmonious society is to be built. When I emphasize the ideal of character in this book, I am not thinking of any narrow or separate human trait, nor am I denying the importance of the intellectual phases of the college experience; I am only insisting that educated men and women should possess that type of personality in which the dictates of reason and the mandates of morality blend to form an orderly and compulsive pattern of living. In short, this book contends that the liberal college must help its students to attain a complete, unselfish, and workable theory of life. I frankly admit the desire to show my reader the glory and nobility of the cultural tradition. The call to college is a call to romance, sacrifice, and courage. The youth who contemplates the attainment of a college degree only in terms of practical and material benefits misses entirely the true significance of higher learning. A college career should not be a routine course of study but an exciting spiritual crusade. The real bachelor of arts is not merely an individual who has passed satisfactorily four years of academic

6

studies. He is one to whom an understanding and appreciation of human knowledge has changed humdrum existence into an exhilarating adventure. The true graduate of a cultural college will know how to make a livelihood, but he will have learned, above all things, the secret of a joyful, creative, and socially constructive life. Underlying all of the liberal arts is a fundamental spiritual attainment — *The Art of Living*.

2. *The Arts of a Liberal Education*

As the foreword indicates, this book is divided into four parts, and each part discusses one aspect of the art of living. These four constituents of a virile and comprehensive liberal perspective are (I) *The Art of Self-Discovery*, (II) *The Art of Self-Discipline*, (III) *The Art of Self-Development*, and (IV) *The Art of Self-Denial*. The first art, *self-discovery*, reflects the teachings of the cultural tradition concerning the dignity and authority of the individual human being. Faith in individual personality is the supreme inspiration to be derived from the college experience. The second art, *self-discipline*, represents the influence of the exactions of rigorous logical thinking. The whole character of a student is affected by the extent of his obedience to the rigorous rules of learning. The third art, *self-development*, bespeaks the value of a fund of knowledge in the student's personal growth. The curricular offerings of the laboratory, the library, and the lecture room all combine to give him the resources for abundant mental enjoyment and effective practical behav-

7

ior. Finally, the fourth art, *self-denial*, reveals the effects of a college education upon the student's social responses. No person can truly be called a liberally educated person if he lacks a sympathetic understanding of the baffling problems of societal life. As I have already insisted, no cultural outlook can be complete which does not include a passion to promote the total welfare of mankind. If the college of today is to command the imagination and loyalty of youth, it must present a challenge as lofty as the voice of the church and as dramatic as the call to war.

3. *The College Perspective*

For three centuries the American arts colleges have proudly cast their light and learning upon every sphere of national life. Holy mounts of vision, they acquired early a transcendent glamour which long dazzled the ordinary citizen of the country. This prestige reflected the connection between the first colleges of America with the old and famous universities of Oxford and Cambridge. Our colonial colleges had a religious motivation and purpose which also gave them a glorified status. Until recently college presidents were extolled as oracles of universal truth; college professors were revered as high priests of a mystery cult; and college graduates were honored as the divinely privileged custodians of the wisdom of the race.

In the last few decades, however, the clouds of glory, which long enveloped the colleges in mystic splendor, have been rapidly vanishing, and the ivory towers of our academic castles are now open to the vulgar inspection of every gaper. The mists which once enwrapped the citadel of higher learning with the romantic illusions of an aristocratic tradition are fast disappearing in the burning heat of a wartime climate. The decrease in the influence of the churches in educational programs, the rise of scientific studies, and the development of industrialism in the American way of life have all produced the demand for democratic, practical, and secular programs of education.

There have always been rifts in the aura of sanctity which has crowned the colleges, but during the last twenty-five years the process of disenchantment has been merciless and sweeping. In the postwar era of disillusionment the invectives against the hypocrisy and foolishness of higher education in America were blatant enough to gratify the most brutal muckraker. The cynical polemic against the boom-era bilge of the American college was softened to some extent by the fact that our industrial and political activities were also subject to cruel attack, but no sentimental defense could negate the stern reality that the voice of Parnassus had lost its profundity and power.

Much of the current distrust of liberal education is due to the conflicts of opinion among college administrators and professors. The debates between the religionists and the secularists, the disciplinarians and the progressives, the intellectualists and the vocationalists, have aroused misgivings in the eye of the public regarding the validity of higher education. How can

9

the man on the street have any definite conception of the aim of college education when educators themselves dispute so vigorously concerning objectives and methods? Just now the campuses are alive with controversies about the new experiments in general education, the separation of the student program into junior and senior divisions, the new stress upon personnel work and guidance, and the importance of the foreign languages and higher mathematics in the educative process. Disillusioning to the average citizen as these professional arguments are, they do indicate that the colleges are alive to the changes in society at large. Controversies among educators reflect their earnest desire to make education sensitive to new times and conditions. When one considers the revolutionary changes which have recently occurred in the social process, one is amazed that the college has not lost more of its traditional unity and purpose.

My purpose is not to bewail the cause and future of the arts college. On the contrary, I affirm my earnest faith in the efficacy and permanence of liberal education in the development of American life and culture. In spite of its many variations and controversies, the college is a civilizing influence whose merits have a right to be recognized by persons in all classes and all callings. I trust that this book will indicate why American undergraduates should appreciate the ideals of the cultural life. Only when students themselves believe in liberal education can arguments for the college be convincing to the population at large. And only as long as the American people as a

10

whole maintain their faith in cultural ideals will our nation preserve a democracy worth saving. The modern youth who with supercilious cynicism contemns what his parents cherished as college spirit will never know the splendid satisfactions of co-operative social living.

4. *The Need for a Philosophy of Liberal Education*

The average high-school graduate knows a great deal about the social and athletic events which make a college year exciting, but he has only a vague and confused appreciation of the academic curriculum. Without some preliminary knowledge of the foundations and methods of the instructional fields, the beginning student is likely to enter upon his course with indifference and prejudice. Only the freshman who understands with insight and regards with enthusiasm the essential meanings of human knowledge can expect to become a truly educated person.

There are many stimulating and profitable pursuits on a campus besides courses of study, but fortunate is the student who combines curricular and extracurricular activities in one energetic, coherent educational program. Fortunate also is the student who is able to relate his curricular experiences to the off-campus world of practical affairs. To the college man or woman whose academic responses suggest a background of wide experience, education offers its finest rewards. Liberal education, no less than applied education, is education for life.

11

College studies cannot long command the interest and industry of the student who takes his courses without definite and compelling reasons. There are many causes of failure in scholastic work — poor health, excessive outside employment, inadequate high-school preparation, too many extracurricular activities, slovenly study habits, and so on—but more powerful than any of these is the disbelief in scholarship which characterizes the mind of the average failing student. The undergraduate has great respect for courses which have a direct vocational significance. The student in a premedical course schedules without reservation chemistry and zoology, the student in commerce acknowledges readily the value of accounting and economics, and the student in journalism admits willingly the importance of composition and history. What irritates the typical freshman is a list of required or recommended courses in subjects which, in his opinion, have no possible relation to everyday living. "Why take a foreign language, or astronomy, or philosophy?" he asks in exasperation. A class hour in one of these subjects must be extraordinarily lively if the mood of revolt is to be dispelled.

The college will never challenge the imagination and loyalty of young people until it can convince them that every part of the total curriculum is important for the abundant life. The value of the so-called cultural studies must be demonstrated as clearly as the value of the so-called practical sciences if college education is to merit the approval of youth. No longer can educators and parents make young people study for the sake of moral discipline or social prestige. Better claims than these must be made for liberal education if the modern American student is to take his college program with sincerity and zeal. In short, if a college would maintain the respect and devotion of its students, it must have a wise and vigorous philosophy of education.

5. *The Spiritual Basis of the Liberal-Arts College*

During recent years the colleges of liberal arts have overemphasized the superficial and mechanical features of education. They have brought into their processes of administration and instruction the procedures of the vocational and professional schools. Too many cultural colleges turn out standardized B.A.'s with the speed and efficiency of manufacturing plants. Students are weighed, tested, and classified like products on an assembly line. Hosts of professors, restricted to the policies and methods of mass production, have lost their originality and zest. Educational experimenters have disclosed with amazing accuracy what students *can* do and *do* do in their studies, but there are few interpreters who tell students what they *ought* to do. Education, in becoming realistic and pragmatic, has lost sight of its right and obligation to be idealistic and humanistic. In following procedures based on statistical averages it has forgotten the claims and capacities of the individual seeker of knowledge. Teaching, once a glorious opportunity to enflame youth to a

13

radiant idealism, is now all too often a dreary job in which weary workmen, to get a rise or a promotion, grind out obtuse monographs which only a few spiritless souls like themselves will ever read.

Colleges cannot afford to neglect the advantages of technical and methodological improvements in their programs; but what higher education needs today more than anything else is an exhilarating emotionalism which will make its creeds convincing and its codes compelling. If the liberal-arts college is to be the leader in adventurous programs for a better social order, it must speedily abandon its contemporary moods of moral and intellectual apathy and smugness. The one-time faith in cultural idealism which, like a fiery beacon, inspired youth with audacious and sacrificial devotion now resembles a flickering jack-o'-lantern casting pale beams of sweetness and light. If the college of liberal arts does not drastically recapture its historic passion for truth and righteousness, to some other educational institution will be entrusted the intellectual and ethical inspiration of young people. No less than a nation of lost ideals, a college without vision is sure to perish.

If my readers object that I am insisting too strongly on the spiritual aspects of college life, I reply that the only educational doctrine which is permanently practical and profitable is the one which audaciously meets the demands of human nature at its best. To have faith in the education of humanity is to believe in an enterprise which demands the truest and strongest courage. If social progress through liberal education

14

is a vain fancy, then the beliefs of religion in the triumph of brotherhood and freedom are empty sentimentalisms. If faith in cultural education is a futile emotionalism, then the drama of civilization is a farce and the epic of Christianity only a pretty myth. Professor A. N. Whitehead has proclaimed the spirit of adventure to be the dynamic of social advancement. I know of no better way for America to cultivate the adventurous mood than by pursuing the educational vision of a responsible, free, and enlightened people.

Youth is entering upon an era which will demand to the utmost the spirit of altruism and devotion. Educators do not need to worry, however, about the loyalty of our young — youth always has the passion to be loyal. The responsibility of educators is to help the rising generation to select goals which will challenge the noblest efforts of the human spirit. It is a wonderful thing for a college to turn out well-informed graduates, intellectually eligible for the most exacting demands of the best professional schools; but it is tremendously more important that a college also have a flaming moral zeal for justice and truth. There are thousands of students who will be successful because they have the necessary technological knowledge to control the outward circumstance, but only a few will have the wisdom which comes with an appreciation of inner spiritual power. Few will have that faith which is more precious than any technology — the divine insight that makes men free. If my emphasis on spiritual values seems too pious and otherworldly, I can but assert my conviction that only an idealistic

15

type of education can produce an outlook wise enough and strong enough to safeguard the democratic way of life. American homes, churches, industries, and political institutions need for their preservation a citizenry educated in loyalty and courage as well as in knowledge.

6. *The Importance of Personality*

There are many ways to measure the moral and cultural excellence of a nation. No way has been more profound or more instructive than that of evaluating a nation in terms of its success in fulfilling what reflective man has pre-eminently believed to be the ultimate meaning of human society. Social progress, as the greatest interpreters of civilization have affirmed, is the eternal spirit of humanity becoming objective in the lives and institutions of particular peoples. Throughout the ages of thought one ideal has been repeatedly extolled as the supreme aim of civilization. The goal of social evolution, in the light of this dominant vision, is the emergence of a society in which belief in the sacredness of human individuality shall become the motivating conviction of all conduct. No state can possess a nobler ideal than that of producing as many free, happy, intelligent, and responsible personalities as possible. Civilization must mean the increasing development of independent, creative, moral selves or it will mean worse than nothing.

However inspiring it may be to believe in the divine origin of such great social institutions as the Church

16

and the State, and however awesome the complicated machinery of their extensive operations may be, the most convincing argument for their continuance is the contribution which these organizations make to the personal experience of private human selves. Talk as we will about the glories of our socialized and mechanized age, the fact remains that individual persons are the only creative centers of the intelligence and good will necessary for the maintenance of modern community life. Communities cannot feel, suffer, hope, think; only individuals can hate injustice, appreciate order, or make plans. The great psychologist William James was profoundly correct in his insight that "the person in the singular," and not the social institution, is "the more fundamental phenomenon" of modern life. "Underneath all, individuals," sang Walt Whitman, and displayed in his singing the essence of true philosophy and sound politics.

The state is "the individual writ large," and the secret of good government and education is to respect and develop the rights and capacities of the many. The concept "government of the people, by the people, and for the people" still remains man's loftiest and wisest political vision. A government may be ever so benevolent and just; but when it presumes to relieve its citizens of the joy and task of creating their own cultural and political ideals, the nation loses something of its virility. The era of rampant and predatory individualism is over, both in economic and in political life; but collectivistic methods for society should be welcomed only upon one important condition. This

17

proviso is the requirement that the emerging systems of business and government shall not be regarded as ends in themselves but as means for enriching the lives of individual selves. Whether state capitalism, socialism, fascism, or communism will arise out of the collapse of the old capitalistic individualism, the new order will have to recognize the civic and intellectual liberties of the masses if it is to acquire the social vitality and the moral authority to endure. In the midst of danger and disaster anti-democratic government may be necessary as an emergency measure of recovery; but if it does not widely encourage the voluntary interest and intelligent participation of its citizenry, it will not long continue.

The task of thoughtful persons today is not to decry the rise of socialized forms of industrial and political life. Socialization based upon expert technological and sociological knowledge is imperative if we are to save ourselves from the wastefulness, injustice, and demagoguery of rampant individualism. The task of our reflective citizens just now is to see that the movement toward a socialized order commands the sympathetic and intelligent appreciation of the multitudes. Ordinary citizens, of course, will not provide the inventive and executive genius necessary for the construction of the new and better social system, but they will furnish the popular approval without which the best reformers can never succeed. The graduates of liberal colleges cannot all be leaders, but they can all give their intellectual and moral endorsement to the innovations which promise greater happiness and progress for man. If college men and women fear and fight reformation in industry and government, the masses can hardly be expected to welcome new and better ways.

7. *The Ideal of Individuality in Education*

The problem of individual personality in our national life reduces itself to this pointed query: Can education give to the ordinary American citizen an appreciative understanding of the meanings and burdens of modern complex society? To put the question another way: Can Americans, as a people, transcend the influence of competitive industry, departmentalized education, partisan politics, sectarian religion, biased journalism, and class antagonism to the extent that they may acquire a disinterested, synoptic, unified, and creative social vision? In a word, can democracy be trusted to lead the nation out of injustice and chaos into righteousness and order?

To these momentous questions I declare that a confident affirmative answer is possible. The ground of this confidence is the enthusiastic faith of our leading educators in the intellectual and moral potentialities of the average man. However weak the belief in economic and political democracy may be in America today, our trust in democratic principles of education seems to be stronger than ever. Present-day educational authorities do not believe that all persons should be given the same amounts or the same kinds of educa-

19

tion; modern biology, psychology, and sociology have shown us conclusively that the idea of absolute intellectual equality is a fanciful myth. But contemporary educators do believe that much of the mental inferiority among our people is due to removable physiological and social handicaps, and they constantly plead for medical, economic, and legislative programs which will better the intellectual opportunities and capacities of the underprivileged sections of our population. That society is under a sacred obligation to help the masses to obtain their full and just rights to educational enlightenment is one of the dominant ideals of American educational doctrine.

Despite the shameful claptrap and petty politics in the management of many of our schools, and despite the mediocrity of many of our underpaid and uninspired teachers, the educational system is by far the most influential and respected force making for free ethical personality in America today. No group is more alert to the national importance of an intelligent and responsible populace than is the educational profession. While many economists, political advisers, editors, sociologists, and other students of social phenomena urge the establishment of a collectivistic society, educators are insisting that the new socialized order shall promote what John Dewey has called " the recovery of composed, effective and creative individuality." Educators in their public utterances often talk so fervently about the need of new economic and political contexts for human life that we ignore their routine, quiet, persistent labors in the classroom to

20

produce individual thinkers who have the intelligence and courage to bring about the desired social conditions. In spite of their enthusiastic recognition of the influence of environmental and hereditary forces in human development, educators have always found much to favor in the traditional thesis of religion that the best possible social gospel is the one which preaches individual salvation. When all is said, education must deal with minds, and minds occur only in separate, private selves. The implications and values of education extend throughout the entire social community, but the basic location of the educative process is, after all, in individual and personal experience.

Acknowledgment of the concept of individuality in education is disclosed in many of the newer emphases and methods. The old spirit of " take it or leave it " is fast disappearing from the attitude of the teachers. It is increasingly becoming the business of the teacher to make the student *like* to take it. There is a painstaking effort in our better schools to teach in as stimulating, interesting, and helpful a manner as possible. Individualized curricula, project activities, co-operative assignments, tasks demanding creative and critical work, clinical demonstrations, radio and movie programs, lectures by famous men and women, substitution of discussion periods for the old lecture-recitation system, personal conferences, interviews in the homes of teachers, orientation courses, education combined with travel and field work — these and scores of other instructional devices are making the enterprise of learning more fascinating, useful, and vital.

21

Very important in recent educational procedure is the development of personnel services. Instructional methods and curricular offerings now reflect the nature and needs of students. The educator in the standard American college is no longer ignorant concerning the capacities and interests of the individual members of the student body. Psychological tests to ascertain the intelligence of students, tests on reading abilities, tests to discover moral and social traits, and many other scientific devices are used to study the personalities and potentialities of students. Placement tests enable the administrative officers to place students in classes suited to their abilities; health examinations suggest remedial care which will improve their physical proficiency; and vocational guidance provides useful information concerning the requirements and opportunities in the various life careers. The undergraduate who avails himself of the personnel services of his college can receive individualized guidance which will improve his chances for success, not only in the academic field but also in the later vocational civic life.

Testifying further to the efficacy of the democratic vision in education is the fact that educational activities and opportunities have been extended far beyond the traditional period of the teaching of children and youth. Schools for infants and very young children are becoming increasingly numerous and popular. More significant, however, than all the other recent educational developments is the rapid growth in adult education. Lodges, trade unions, women's groups, libraries, church organizations, luncheon clubs, and many other societies are becoming more and more available to teachers and scholars as agencies of public instruction. Night schools, labor colleges, part-time universities, and other educational institutions organized especially for the adult student are additional testimony to the vitality of the democratic ideal in American life. Finally, the tendency in our old-established institutions of higher learning to treat students as responsible citizens charged with important social and political obligations is rapidly replacing the historic notion that undergraduates cannot be expected to be anything more than immature, care-free youth.

The growing enrollment in schools of all types, the trend of educated young people toward professional or political activities, and the decided tendency of teachers and students alike to regard the educative process more critically and conscientiously, together with many other factors, plainly show that the American people are keenly aware that the dictum of H. G. Wells to the effect that the future is a race between education and catastrophe is no idle jest. Stimulating the entire movement toward better public education is the increase in leisure time which the machine age has made possible. Educators, social workers, and public officials are turning their attention seriously to the problem of profitable forms of mental and physical recreation for men and women who in factory, office, or store bear the burdens of the day. We are at last beginning to realize that it is foolishness to educate

23

the children in social idealism if the world which they must eventually enter is controlled by adults in whom the light of learning has grown dim.

8. *The Significance of Freedom*

The development of intelligent and responsible persons as the goal of liberal education has no meaning unless men and women can be regarded as free, self-determining individuals.

Scholars in religion, philosophy, and education have been fundamentally right in their endorsement of the historic thesis that free will is the basis of wisdom and morality. Such concepts as praise and blame, guilt and sin, heroism and cowardice, goodness and evil, are meaningless unless human beings can voluntarily choose the goals and methods of their conduct. If a man does not have a will which reflects his own ideals, he can never be a truly rational or responsible person. Unless there are responses which proceed from free choice in the face of alternatives, then such ideals as freedom of speech, civil liberties, conscience, democracy, and liberalism are futile and deceptive hopes.

The ideal of moral freedom is directly opposed to the doctrine of determinism, which maintains that all events in man's physical life are completely explainable in terms of the mechanistic and external forces of heredity and environment. The moral theory assumes that in the determinations of human behavior man's own intelligence has a selective and constructive role to

24

play. No exponent of moral freedom believes, of course, that an individual is capable through sheer power of the will to do anything he wishes; such a belief would be the acceptance of occultism and caprice. The free-willer readily admits that there is a good deal of truth in the determinist's position. Even the stanch believer in free will seeks for himself and his family the best possible physical, biological, and cultural living conditions. The defender of moral freedom, in short, believes that man is most free when he recognizes the conditioning stimuli of human behavior, in order to employ them for the realization of the highest human values. The will, as free, is not an isolated, spontaneous activity; it is the total self, manipulating, in the light of intelligent moral purpose, the conditions in which it finds itself. The view of will as a separate, self-existing power, transcending the other psychological constituents of personality, is a vestige of the now obsolete faculty psychology. The volitional experience to the contemporary psychologist is one phase of man's continuous, unified conscious life.

From earliest history mankind has recognized the importance of freedom. All the conflicts of human beings from the primitive feuds to the competition of modern commercial groups have been, in the opinions of the participants, struggles for a freer life. From savage magic to scientific technology the one continuous aim of the human spirit has been to rid itself of bondage and restraint. The strifes of today between dictatorial and democratic forms of government and

25

between collectivistic and individualistic systems of industry reflect divergent roads to freedom in the minds of their respective proponents. The rivalries between classicism and modernism in the arts, absolutism and relativism in ethics, naturalism and theism in religion, mechanism and purpose in science, all reduce to different conceptions of the nature and function of freedom. Militarists and pacifists, communists and anarchists, radicals and traditionalists, all believe they are promoting the cause of freedom in the social order. Only a fool or a brute would venture to ignore or disparage the deep-seated love of freedom in the heart of the race. In performance, tyrants may enslave their people, but in propaganda they are very careful to praise and promise the blessings of freedom. In the name of liberty, man has produced his noblest works and has committed his foulest deeds. The profound German philosopher Wilhelm Hegel was fundamentally correct in his central thesis that in the progress of freedom history finds its meaning and purpose.

The strife between different systems of thought and action is not over the desirability but over the definition of freedom. The problem of the social interpreter today is not to inculcate this spiritual power in mankind but to give it rational explanation and moral direction. The desire for liberty is a basic and universal impulse in the original nature of man. And it is, furthermore, a longing which the dehumanizing forces of modern mechanical civilization have not suppressed or diminished. The zeal for liberty must be

26

intelligent and practical if it is to become an instrument of social progress and harmony. In these days of conflicting conceptions of freedom, we need, among many possible definitions, an ideal of the free life which will meet the loftiest demands of goodness and truth. No country can ever become a "land of the noble free" unless it possesses a noble philosophy of freedom. No nation will ever develop free personalities, free governments, free schools, free religions, or free arts until it attains a rational and workable theory of freedom itself.

When we investigate the situations in which individuals realize their freedom, we discover that human selfhood is largely a product of nonpersonal influences. The intelligence with which a person employs these influences will determine, to a great extent, the nature and adequacy of his behavior. The great task of education is to show how these forces can be made the liberators and not the destroyers of mankind. These basic and influential factors are of three main types: *physical*, *biological*, and *sociological*. Let us briefly examine each of them.

9. *The Physical Environment of Man*

There is an outstanding tendency in contemporary thought to depreciate the nobility of man. Instead of emphasizing the human individual as a self-important and self-directive being, the present-day interpreter of selfhood idealizes the environment of man. Today the fascination which was traditionally attached to the

27

concept of the human soul has been transferred to the impersonal conditions of the spiritual person. Man's worth, in contemporary thought, is mainly a merit obtained by his relations to various situations. We subscribe to a scientific pantheism which is almost as destructive of human individuality as the mystical monisms of the past.

The human spirit depends upon impersonal factors for its continuance and purpose. We may talk as we will about the glories of the creative human mind, but the materialistic environmentalist will soon remind us that without certain physical and chemical surroundings there would be no personal, conscious life at all. In fact, without carbon compounds — the carbohydrates, the fatty acids, and the amino acids — there would not be any life at all. Furthermore, without the stimuli of the material universe there would be no sense perceptions; without sense perceptions, no meditations and reflections; and without these higher processes of thought, no art, philosophy, or science.

An important school of thinkers has maintained that the lives of individuals and of peoples are chiefly to be explained in terms of their physical environment. Human history, according to this group, is mainly the result of physico-geographical forces. The direction of civilization is accounted for by such factors as climate, soil fertility, availability of minerals, water supply, contour, and the possibilities of commerce and communication. The early civilizations of Egypt, Mesopotamia, and China are explainable by the fact that they developed in fertile river valleys. The in-

tellectual and artistic glory of Greece is intelligible
only when we appreciate the blue skies and beautiful
scenery of this favored land. The temperamental differences of peoples in the north and the south of Europe,
as well as the psychical differences of the north and the
south of our own country, are to be explained largely
in terms of climatic and geographic contrasts. According to some scientists who study the geographical
influences on man, mountaineers necessarily differ
from plainsmen in their attitudes toward life, and
even the weather is regarded as having an effect on
the number of suicides and crime.

The discoveries in recent astronomy have also had
their effect upon notions of human selfhood. The
change from the Ptolemaic to the Copernican conception of the universe deprived men of a proud place
as the inhabitants of the centrally located heavenly
body, but now knowledge of the magnitude of the
sidereal universe has reduced the spatial prestige of
our home planet to complete insignificance. With the
naked eye one can see about four thousand stars;
but with one of the largest telescopes several million
stars may be viewed. Our sun is but one star, and a
small one at that, in a galaxy of one to two million
fellow stars. Four years are required for light to pass
from the nearest star to our planet. How modest a
place, after all, has man in the mammoth cosmos and
how natural the attitude that the human soul is a
transient trifle! It is small wonder that a philosophy of
serene, but pathetic, resignation has arisen in the light
of our knowledge of great magnitudes. Aesthetic awe

29

toward the infinite spaces has taken the place of ethical adventurousness in the face of colossal natural forces. We are in danger of becoming astronomical mystics.

10. *Biological Foundations of Selfhood*

Man as an organism is a marvelous creature. Digestive, circulatory, excretory, nervous, endocrine, neuro-muscular, and several other systems unite in their functioning to sustain his total life process. A superficial enumeration indicates the complexity and intricacy of his organic parts: more than two hundred bones, almost seven hundred muscles, twenty feet of digestive tubing, a hundred thousand miles of blood vessels, about two and one-half trillion red blood cells, and four million white blood cells. Yet man is a very recent and a very young feature in the thousand million years of organic evolution. He has hardly begun to develop the powers with which he is so richly endowed. Large areas of his brain cells are still undeveloped and suggest possibilities beyond our present imagination. And, since his conduct is largely determined by the nature of the stimuli that affect his reacting mechanism, we may expect the increased control of man's environment through the instruments of science to produce the kinds of reaction which will be most conducive to human happiness and progress.

The forces in man's biological nature determine largely the types of acts which he performs. Our native traits, as instincts and emotions, can be developed and specialized, but they cannot be totally eradicated.

30

Personality is, to a large extent, the organization of acquired habits, but our inherited capacities determine how far the attainment of personal habits shall go. The moral character which a person possesses is, to a large extent, the result of the direction of the native impulses which give a dynamic urge to life. Two psychological doctrines disparage the reality of the spirit, namely, *behaviorism* and *Freudianism*. These doctrines neglect, if they do not actually deny, the place of free choice in human activity. Behaviorism would substitute for such terms as *soul*, *spirit*, *ego*, and *consciousness* the term *reaction* as the best notion for the explanation of man. The behaviorist is interested in the prediction and control of human conduct, and believes that if mechanical categories are applied to the study of human beings man's activity can be conditioned as successfully as the motions of a physical machine. The Freudian psychologists, or followers of Sigmund Freud, explain personality in terms of non-rational factors. They believe that in the lowest psychical processes lie the driving and dominating forces of life. The power of these subconscious forces is not found in moments of reflective activity but when the reason as censor is off guard, as in dream experiences. When these basic desires are thwarted, we develop emotional states of fear and inefficiency, called complexes. Persons suffering because of repressed desires often develop what is generally known as an inferiority complex. The desire which has received most attention is the sex wish, or libido; and art, literature, religion, and even science and industry have been ex-

31

plained as sublimated expressions of sexual desire. It must be recognized, however, that recent psychoanalytic doctrines, as Freudian theories are sometimes called, treat the sex impulse as just one among many driving appetites of man.

Recently we have learned that a great deal of man's psychological nature is determined by the chemical constituents of the blood. Changes in the bodies and minds of individuals are produced by variations in the secretions of thyroid, adrenal, and other ductless glands. For example, man's valor may be stimulated by an increase in the sugar content of the blood, an increase which is produced by the secretion of adrenalin. Including all the biological factors which influence personality is the total health of an individual. Man's disposition, attitudes, and achievements depend largely upon his freedom from illness and pain. No challenge can be more stirring to the college youth of today than the call to join the ranks of the biological and medical scientists who are trying to destroy the bacteria and viruses which yearly bring suffering and death to thousands of men and women. No less important is the appeal to eradicate the occupational diseases and the industrial accidents which impede the advancement of man.

11. *Sociological Factors in Human Response*

Besides the physical and biological situations which influence the development of man's cultural nature, there is, in the third place, the effect of social environment on individuals. Most direct and lasting of all social influences is family life. The contemporary problems of divorce, child labor, crowded living arrangements, and so on, are all reflected in the character of the individual citizen. The community also exerts a tremendous influence on the individual. We are all aware of the differences in persons from the country, the small town, and the metropolitan city. Again, the spirit of the age is a determining factor in human development. People who have lived in exceptional epochs of civilization have found their thoughts and enthusiasms determined by the intellectual movements of their day. The enlightened era of Periclean Athens, the Renaissance of Italy, the Industrial Revolution of England, were all periods of thought and activity which influenced the consciousness of the individual man. And who will deny the tragic effect of the totalitarian political environment on the free spirit of European peoples under dictatorships?

The machine age, again, dominates the thought and life of contemporary man. The machine is being decried as the enemy of all that is free and fine in personality. Many interpreters of present culture indict the materialism, mammonism, and monotony of modern industrial life. We might elaborate the effect of the newspapers, the radio, the movies, advertising, and other modern agencies of communication upon the individual mind. Such an elaboration is not necessary, however, as we all know too well the standardized and propagandized state of the American spirit.

33

And when we consider the moral context of contemporary life, we have to admit that the self in its pursuit of perfection is beset with grievous impediments. Instances of social obstacles to proficient personality could be almost indefinitely continued: unemployment, poverty, illiteracy, industrial strife, shallow amusements, war, crime, absence of religious education — all these and scores of other social deficiencies today cry out that America is not yet the land of the free or the home of the brave.

The above considerations lead us to acknowledge without hesitancy that a man is in a large measure subject to the laws of the physical, biological, and sociological orders. We admit that human beings are, to a great degree, animals, even machines. If we did not recognize that personality is the result of many external forces, then we should have to deny the value of food, drink, shelter, churches, schools, and all the instruments and conveniences of life. We cannot but realize that man is a physiological organism, living in a physical, temporal world, and not a heavenly being exempt from all the necessities and influences of temporal existence. The wise college student will regard highly the influence of health conditions, environmental factors, and social relations on his academic purpose and success.

In part III of this book the teachings of the natural and social sciences regarding human behavior are fully outlined. Knowledge of these curricular areas is not merely an intellectual treat for a privileged few. However fascinating scientific studies may be for the minority now permitted to enjoy them, their primary function is to provide ideas and instruments to make all mankind intelligent and free.

12. *The Spirit of Man*

Man is not only a biological agency, determined exclusively by naturalistic and mechanical forces. When all is said, the influence of heredity and environment are conditions, not causes, of human destiny. Physical and political forces may mold, but they cannot make, a soul. They may shake, but they cannot break, the indomitable spirit of man. What we need today is less emphasis on man as descended from the animal, and more stress on what he can *become*.

The spiritual and creative influences of freedom have been disregarded in our exclusive attention to freedom as control of circumstance. The traditional doctrine of natural rights, which locates the sources of freedom in physical and social conditions, has so monopolized our thinking that the notion of freedom as the expression of inner, creative spirit has passed from the vocabulary of popular speech.

Contemporary thinkers who take an instrumental and practical view of freedom deny all cosmic and eternal features of man. In their judgment, to be free is to enjoy and develop the intellectual, physiological, and social responses in human behavior; freedom, they say, comes through the control and use of environmental and biological forces which condition the progress and happiness of the race. This humanistic and

35

utilitarian definition of freedom deprives the term of its fullest meaning. The practical thinker mistakes the evidences and effects of freedom for freedom itself. Freedom is not merely a word to denote a certain type of human reaction, however enjoyable or successful the reaction may be. Freedom is that dynamic force which pushes man on deliberately to pursue a life of enjoyment and success.

Experimentation, organization, legislation, and education can contribute to the cultivation of the free spirit, but the final source of freedom is not in sociological instruments. Defining freedom as liberty from restraint and bondage may arouse the downtrodden to revolution, but revolutionists themselves must develop a positive ideal of freedom before they will ever realize the abundant experience of free living. The really free man is one who is free *for*, and not merely free *from*, the dangers and difficulties of existence. Man when he is at his best is free, but freedom at its best far transcends the human. In the view of the idealist, to the mind of the cosmos we must look for the ultimate meaning of freedom.

The fundamental nature of freedom is spirit, and spirit is the principle of creativity which invades every part and parcel of the universe. Throughout the centuries philosophers have proclaimed this conception. In the fire of Heraclitus, the Eros of Plato, the Logos of the Fourth Gospel, the Monads of Leibnitz, the Will of Kant, Fichte, Hegel, and Schopenhauer, and the Vital Impetus of Bergson the cosmic and dynamic character of freedom is revealed. Freedom is the life and energy of the world. Freedom cannot be reduced to mechanical organization, mathematical formulation, or legal regulation. So far as their capacity to depict the essence of freedom is concerned, all languages are dead languages. Pragmatists and humanists emphasize, and rightly so, the adventurous tone of man's behavior; idealists go further and give these features of human experience cosmic proportions. Professor Royce sums up this whole thesis when he affirms that man is free because he is a part of the world-creator. But a word of both warning and assurance: Participation in the great spiritual freedom is neither inevitable nor compulsory. We are not predestined by a World Mind or Force to experience the cultural ideals which have impelled the race to progress. Appreciation of the creative motives of civilization comes only with individual choice and self-determination. The cosmic influences toward freedom are available to all, but no man can be forced by God or government to accept them against his private will. One of the great consequences of a liberal education is the development of an intelligent enthusiasm for the challenges of freedom.

This conception of freedom is frankly theoretical, but it is not a vain fancy. The notion of a free and creative universe which can be expressed in finite experience is an ideal; but it is an ideal desperately needed as a tonic to our faith in the significance and vitality of democracy. It is a type of freedom which, with its emphasis on the inner spiritual life, we find in the experiences of the poet, seer, prophet, or saint.

Not in the impersonal observation of external objects, however beautiful and orderly their relationships may be, not in the exhilaration of a blind, irrational subservience to an autocratic social will, but in the deep, inner feelings of private devotion, profound sorrow, aesthetic contemplation, romantic love, religious mysticism, and in similar profound experiences of the heart, we discover the real arguments for human freedom. The realm of personal freedom, like the kingdom of heaven, is within, and only the deep responses of the soul can truly or fully reveal the free spirit of man. Liberal education is education which recognizes the importance of these hidden resources of personal experience. Liberal education does not deny the importance of knowledge of man's outward behavior and his external environment. It does insist, however, that — in a day when the emphasis is on the external and material aspects of experience — art, literature, music, philosophy, and religion must occupy their rightful place in the educated man's outlook.

In part III of this book the objectives of the humanities in the college curriculum are discussed. No less than the scientific curricula, the humanities must contribute to the self-realization of every individual in the social community and not merely to the intellectual gratification of an aristocratic few. If the humanities are not for all humanity, the ideal of a spiritual and cultural democracy is a pathetic delusion.

Before an American can fully cherish the principles and merits of democracy, he must appreciate clearly the implications of totalitarian absolutism. He must even recognize the constructive aspects of totalitarianism, and ascertain how and where they might be employed to advantage in the democratic process. Let us notice the chief dogmas of the contemporary German dictatorship. In the main, they reflect also the absolutisms of Italy and Japan.

13. *The Cultural Effects of Totalitarianism*

When one examines the ideology of Nazism, three cultural principles stand out: (a) the ideal of destiny; (b) the ideal of unity; (c) the ideal of sufficiency. Let us notice the effects of these three ideals of the totalitarian mind. We shall indicate, in the case of each ideal, its religious, educational, and moral significance.

By the ideal of destiny I mean the belief that a nation inevitably follows an underlying Force or Will which no individual or group of individuals has the power or right to question or impede. In Germany it expresses itself in the myth of race and in the glorification of the state; it is an irrational surging impetus which carries the movements of an entire people in its sweep.

Carried into religious thought, this ideal of destiny results in a philosophy of grim devotion. The arts of persuasion, the blessings of consolation, and the mood of tolerance, which have always characterized religion at its best, are completely ignored. There are hymns, but they are hymns of hate; there

39

are prayers, but they are prayers of vengeance. Creeds
and theologies based upon reflective debates in ec-
clesiastical councils have no place in this religion, with
its single, absolute faith.

In education the ideal of destiny gives the school
but one purpose — namely, that of glorifying the state
as the final end of human evolution. Propaganda re-
places instruction, and the freedom of liberal scholarship is lost in the emotional exaltation of national
prestige. No more is there a world-wide culture which
reflects the total and lasting human spirit. All art,
literature, and science become the tool of the guardians
of a nationalistic, uncritical culture. There are more
and more schools, for all ages, classes, and places — but
curricula everywhere inculcate the myth of the state.

In morality the ideal of destiny denies the values of
human personality which reside in the principles of
natural rights and civil liberties. Freedom is no
longer self-determination. Action, and not reflection,
becomes the chief mark of the ethical life; it is small
wonder that violence is extolled as the supreme virtue.
Only in brutality can the Nazi forget that he really
is a slave.

The ideal of unity also manifests itself in European
religion, education, and morality.

In religion, unity is realized by the deification of
the leader. The dictator may proclaim himself the
servant of the state, or the subject of a king; but to
the people he is the Messiah, the miracle-worker, or
God incarnate. Even when there is any pretense of
recognizing the significance of Christ in the Christian

40

tradition, Christ is given the character of a war lord. The right of the church, Catholic or Protestant, to any authority in political or economic activity is completely denied. Although religious societies are allowed prerogatives in the realm of the spiritual, Christianity is interpreted as being inferior to the spiritual glory of the national state. There is a Sunday-school song which, paraphrased, expresses the religious unity of a totalitarian nation: "Trust and obey; for there's no other way to be happy in Hitler but to trust and obey."

In education the ideal of unity expresses itself in a folk culture. Literature, music, drama, the dance, and the other arts all tell but one story, and that story is the epic of the nation's history, struggle, power, and destiny. Paramount in the educational drive toward unity is the emphasis upon the strength and principles of youth. Lord Halifax, in addressing the students of Oxford some time ago, said, "The struggle today is not between youth and age, it is between youth and youth." One of the great handicaps of the democratic nations is the fact that their youth, during the past ten years, have been instructed in the arts of peace, while the boys and girls of the dictatorships have been stimulated in every possible way with the glories of war.

The moral expression of the ideal of unity is found in the emphasis upon the well-being of all the people. We must recognize the practical insight of the totalitarian states in extending the benefits of social insurance, adult education, housing projects, universal

41

vacations, country-wide theaters and concerts, national sports and games. The slogans "Strength through joy" and "Beauty of labor" may reflect highly emotional propaganda, but they do represent aims which command the enthusiasm of a people.

Let us now pass to the religious, educational, and moral consequences of the ideal of sufficiency.

The aim to be self-sufficient on all counts had led in religion to a repudiation of other faiths and creeds. Anti-Catholicism, anti-Protestantism, and anti-Semitism have had political and economic causes to be sure, but they also reflect the principle of all dictatorships to be self-supporting in the realms of the spiritual and the cultural as well as in those of the material. In education the ideal of sufficiency has resulted in the emphasis upon the applied arts and sciences. Physics, chemistry, biology, mathematics, history, political science, and even the humanities must somehow or other promote the efficiency and strength of the state. All intellectual and artistic programs which fail to meet the utilitarian standard are denounced as decadent and futile.

Finally, the ideal of sufficiency expresses itself in the repudiation of all moral standards except racial or national power. The virtues of Hebraic and Christian traditions are condemned as the traits of weaklings and fools. Expressing the doctrine that the end justifies the means, lies, deception, and brutality are justified] and praised. War is the noblest arena of moral behavior, and the soldier is the ideal human self.

Taking it for granted that the statements which I

have made regarding the religious, educational, and moral ideals of the German dictatorship are true, what may be said concerning their influence in present European history? I suggest the following possibilities.

In the first place, the cultural perspective of Russia, as more universal than that of Germany, is going to exert a stronger influence in European thought. The Russians have a nationalistic educational outlook, but in arriving at this outlook they accept as material for their own theories the artistic and scientific contributions of the entire human race. In the second place, the Italians have a favorable view of Catholicism and a romantic attitude toward family life which cannot but soften the extreme military point of view of the Nazis toward the church and the home. With the close of the emergency period it is inevitable that the groups now suppressed will become more bold in revolting against the regimentation of the Nazi state. The Protestants, in Lutheranism and Barthianism, still have a theology which places God above Hitler. The Catholics still have the support of a Pope who favors the cultivation of the ancient Christian virtues, and the intellectuals still have their memories and their books which proclaim the triumph of unfettered, universal truth. Furthermore, a nation which allows no criticism of itself and no commendation of others eventually grows self-complacent and vulnerable. A people long trained in the arts of deception ultimately gains the ability to deceive its deceivers. And, finally, propaganda based upon wild emotionalism cannot long maintain its power and its appeal.

43

What effect will the totalitarian ideals and practices have on the democratic way of life? I suggest that the democracies of Great Britain and America will become more *militant*, more *philosophical*, and more *ethical*. In becoming militant they will become more suspicious of the motives and merits of totalitarian dictatorship. They will become more determined to appreciate and promote their own virtues and values, and will fight for the defense of their sacred rights when the principles of the truly liberal human spirit are menaced. Democracies will become more philosophical when they believe, in the spirit of a religious faith, that freedom is just as much a cosmic reality as force, and when they realize that the destiny which shapes our ends is more concerned with the good of actual, individual selves than with the power of a mythical state. And, last of all, democracies will become more ethical when they stop basing their moral sanctions on economic self-interest and on personal happiness. Even more than totalitarian states, democracies have the right to cultivate the heroic and sacrificial virtues. In this moral advance, democracies will appreciate the freedom of the spirit as a cause which constantly exacts the altruistic and audacious devotion of its champions. As long as we keep in our national mind a faith in this kind of democracy, the ideology of the Nazis will not defeat the cultural destiny of the race. And as long as there are youth who need to understand the fundamental principles of this democracy of ours, the liberal college will have a mission to perform.

What is the relation of the ideal of freedom in liberal education to the notion of a good social order, or, in the light of the American political ideal, what has the liberal conception of education to do with the democratic theory of society?

14. *Liberal Education and Democracy*

Spiritual and cultural experiences contribute several distinct values to the democratic way of individual and social life. In the first place, the cultural basis of citizenship provides an enduring program of human development. During the past three centuries the doctrine of rights has been associated too closely with the concept of equality, and the ideal of equality was negative and mechanical. Rights which pertained to every man as a human being were the only ones emphasized, and these represented immunity from self-restraint rather than opportunities for self-realization. Furthermore, these rights were guaranteed by external biological, historical, economic, and political circumstances. Rights had no intrinsic validity or support. Consequently, as new external situations arose which, in theory or in action, made ineffective the concept of universal equality, the doctrine of natural rights lost its influence and appeal. In totalitarian states it has disappeared altogether as a concept representing the prerogatives and values of individual persons.

The right of the individual as maintained in the doctrine of cultural freedom has a special relation to the principle of equality. One has the right to as much

45

freedom as he can appreciate and express in his apprehension of the total cultural movement. There is no one, special, unchanging truth to assimilate; the cosmic purpose is not disclosed in the experience of any one individual, race, age, nation, or religion. The liberalism of the last three centuries emphasized the freedom of the intellectual aristocrat; the communism of today stresses the liberties of the untutored proletariat. The freedom here suggested provides experiences for individuals of all levels of knowledge and achievement. The main appreciation of one's rights comes not from liberties bestowed from without but from the consciousness of one's own right to a life intrinsically valuable in and for itself alone. Freedom, in this sense, is not an equality of abilities and privileges among all men. It is, rather, the prerogative and duty of each individual to realize to the full his own particular potentialities. However different his capacities may be from those of his fellows, a man who fulfills his own opportunities for self-realization and public service will know the meaning and joy of freedom. True equality does not mean uniformity of thought or behavior but freedom for all to fulfill their respective individual purposes. This does not imply a rigorous caste system, because education for real freedom will always bring growth in the quality and extent of human aspirations.

In the second place, the experience of freedom as participation in the dynamic expanding movement of culture promotes the arts of criticism and expression. In the long run, dictatorships are doomed because, in prohibiting opposition to their tenets and deeds, they develop a false and self-defeating sense of security and power. A citizen does get a certain feeling of importance when, as in a totalitarian regime, he conforms to fixed, compulsory dogmas and institutions; such conformity gives him the expansive emotion which participation in any type of larger totality always produces. But this sense of dignity is sentimentally and morally inferior to the consciousness of individual worth which a democratic citizen enjoys when he possesses the legal right to criticize and modify the principles and practices of his state.

Finally, the doctrine of liberal culture as the basis of social behavior provides the best possible approaches to community spirit and purpose. One of the constant threats to dictatorship is the fact that its intellectual and political leadership is resident in a single individual or in a bureaucracy with very few members. This menaces the system in two regards: Revolution is readily available to the masses, who may at any time turn against the dictatorial power and establish a government of their own. Again, the programs and principles of a dictatorship, when resident in a small autocratic minority, may disappear with the death of their proponents. A democratic state established on the thesis of cultural individualism is not seriously subject to these dangers. A society based on the universal recognition of the right of everyone to freedom of thought and expression is not likely to develop the conflicts and polemics which lead to rebellion or nihilism. Open controversy may deter action, and it may cause bitterness of feeling, but, in the long run, it is the best instrument for the expression of the popular will. And where public opinion finds wide expression, revolution is seldom necessary or effective.

In proposing a basis for democracy which will recognize the values of liberal insights, I do not at all depreciate the importance of science, technology, and the practical arts in our complete national perspective. It is admitted freely that the idealist cannot furnish the technical ideas and methodologies for the solution of our baffling modern problems. I only wish to insist that the exponent of the spiritual tradition, of the humanities in learning, presents a view of man's nature and needs without which technologies would have neither meaning nor motivation. In preserving our nation in times of economic and military emergency we must not only know what we are protecting America *from*; we must also be clear as to what we are saving our country *for*. Education must concern itself with both the how and the why of national security and progress.

With dictatorships on the rise and with our own democratic nation manifesting a growing tendency toward collectivism, the theory which we have stated must appear to be a vain dream — a sheer outburst of religious optimism. Maybe so; but democracy's supreme purpose in a world in strife is to keep alive man's faith in the ultimate triumph of spiritual and cultural values. Democracy is worthy of our best plans and programs because it deserves the noblest adventures of our faith.

48

II

THE ART
OF SELF-DISCIPLINE

TECHNIQUES
OF LIBERAL EDUCATION

THE FREE, intelligent, and responsible personality which the preceding pages have been portraying does not come to man as a ready-made gift from heaven. It is developed by the individual through the control of his intellectual and social responses. Learning to be a rational, moral self is man's most serious and exacting obligation, demanding of the learner a constant devotion to the highest educational ideals. It is the supreme function of the liberal college to provide young people with the best possible environment for the learning of these arts of cultural selfhood. The college which will influence most worthily American social life will be the college which inculcates in its students an appreciation of and proficiency in the processes of scholarship. The chief service of the college in promoting a morally and culturally effective democracy is to graduate youth who know how to use their minds with efficiency and enjoyment.

15. *Areas of Academic Experience*

A college student who wishes to cultivate the best intellectual responses during his campus years will seek to understand three educational situations: (1) He will try to develop the most practical and profitable habits of study. Some methods of learning are better

51

than others, and to the attainment of these superior methods the conscientious undergraduate will give his attention and enthusiasm. (2) The student who would gain most from the contents of his courses will develop an appreciative understanding of the fundamental objectives of his curricular program, and he will seek to ascertain the chief interrelationships between the several fields of study. The various studies in the curriculum have different educational aims and values. (3) Through the college course, as an instrument for the development of proficient personality, the student will come to understand his relation to the social problems of the day. Education which is really liberal is not merely for the student's gratification, however lofty the gratifying experiences may be; education must show the relations of knowledge to the world of practical life and the responsibilities of scholarship to a humanity in distress.

The above three areas of the academic experience may be summarized as (1) *the instruments of learning,* (2) *the divisions of knowledge,* and (3) *the responsibilities of scholarship.* The second and third aspects of collegiate education are discussed, in order, in the next two parts of the book. The present part examines the outstanding features of good techniques of studying. In other words, the question immediately before us is this: Under what conditions and according to what methods can the processes of learning most successfully be carried on?

16. *Farewell to Adolescence*

The college period is one of transition from childhood to adulthood. Many academic failures are due to the fact that certain students do not realize that the aims of the college are quite different from those of the high school. Some college freshmen never enter into the spirit of college life because they hang on too assiduously to their high-school associations. They continue to "pal around" with high-school pupils when they should be forming new friendships and interests in their college environment. Entrance into the college experience calls for a break with immaturity and irresponsibility. It means release from the comforting and restraining ministrations of home and family. It demands quick and discriminating adjustments in meeting new and various people. It requires skill and conscientiousness in the management of time and money. It locates the responsibility for academic success almost wholly in the individual student. It points the student's thought toward the necessity of choosing a permanent vocation. It offers the opportunity to develop sex responses which are wholesome and normal instead of those which are base and demoralizing. Finally, the campus experience tends to provoke in the student serious reflections about human purposes and events which should emerge in a philosophy of life.

One can elaborate the significance of college life by contrasting it with the ways of high school. In the first place, work in college is more like the oc-

53

cupation or job of an adult. The college student realizes that if he were not in college he would be busy all day long in an office, factory, or some other place of employment. The thoughtful college student appreciates the fact that thousands of young people of his own age are engaged in hard, exacting labor with little hope of much advancement in position or pay. As in high school, there are many extra-curricular activities on the college campus, but in college it is more difficult to succeed both in studies and in extra-curricular affairs. Again, in college, much more than in high school, standing in one's studies is the criterion of success. Athletics, dramatics, class offices, and student editorships are honored on a college campus, but achievement in these lines is not accorded the high recognition granted to superior rating in scholarship. There are few students who would not prefer a Phi Beta Kappa key (the badge of scholastic distinction) to a letter in football or a cup for oratory. More and more business executives are inquiring at college offices for the academic standing of prospective employees. A record of many extra-curricular attainments is always of great interest to an employer, but without the evidence also of conscientious and satisfactory attention to courses of study an application for a job seldom meets with success. There is reason for this attitude on the part of employers. The college student presumably is in a curriculum which represents his choice of a life vocation. If he does not attend to it with diligence and enthusiasm, it is hardly probable that he will carry on his chosen vocation with any serious devotion. Even if the student has not decided upon his permanent vocation, his curriculum in college is, for the time being, his supreme objective and responsibility. If he does not give it his major loyalty, he and others also may lose confidence in his ability to put first things first.

The freshman in college can easily find excuses for failure to pursue his studies with efficiency and success. He is often fooled by the fact that many college courses have the same titles as certain courses in high school. But he finds out after a time, perhaps too late, that he must read, think, and write a great deal more in the college course. In his high-school course he had a single text; in the college course he may have as many as twenty books to read on the same subject matter. And then there are term papers to write in college. These are not little themes of seven or eight pages; they must be critical and well-organized essays covering fifteen to twenty pages of manuscript. While the youth is in high school his parents see to it that he attends to his studies, and often his teachers urge him to "get down to business." But when he leaves home for college, he is strictly "on his own"; his father or mother will not be around to goad him on, and his professors, although willing to give him helpful counsel, will not feel obligated to make him do his work. Finally, the freshman in college will face a battery of courses which he has never even heard about in high school. In selecting electives for his schedule he will observe, in the catalogue, scores of available courses. Upper-class students, personnel

55

officers, and faculty advisers will be glad to recommend appropriate courses, but the freshman himself must have the desire to schedule subjects which will serve his best educational aims, instead of searching for courses which come at the most convenient hours in the day. The purpose of part III of this book is to present information regarding college courses which will be helpful to students in making beneficial curricular programs.

17. *Making the Grade with Grades*

I have made some statements regarding the comparative value of superior scholarship in courses and of success in extra-curricular activities. In the next few paragraphs I should like to comment further concerning these two phases of the college experience. The importance of distinction in scholarship can be indicated by a discussion of the giving of grades, or marks, on the work which is done in the various courses of study.

Some educators and many students object to the grading of course work by alphabetical or numerical marks. The chief objection is that the system of grades places a false standard of value on academic achievement. The worth of the course is measured by the grade obtained, rather than by the intellectual benefit received. A professor is frequently rated by students according to the grades which he gives, rather than on the basis of his teaching in the classroom. Often, also, the desire for a high grade is the sole motive for

56

superior work. The hope to make a scholarship society, the desire to be eligible for athletics, the fear of probation or dismissal, and other secondary incentives to studying replace the love and joy of studying for its own sake. Finally, grades are occasionally criticized for encouraging the various cheating practices employed by dishonest students. When grades are taken to be the primary criterion of academic achievement, it is small wonder that many students, wholly indifferent to the moral and intellectual standards of scholastic success, regard dishonesty in examinations without any serious disapproval.

There is not space here to argue the merits of the above contentions. The difficulties and dangers of the grading system, however, lie not so much in the grades themselves as in the attitude with which they are regarded by students. No student is compelled to work for high marks; he is perfectly free to study for the very joy of studying and for the intellectual advantage knowledge will give him in years to come. Since most colleges and universities will continue to use grades for the measurement of academic work, I shall indicate some benefits of their use. Whether a student believes in the grading system or not, he should recognize the administrative and educational reasons for its employment.

The use of grades provides a practicable and convenient method for the evaluation of academic performance. Without some sort of marking system the student would be unable to obtain a clear and definite calculation of his educational progress. The student

57

has the right to know whether he is doing what is expected of him, and he is justified in finding out, by the actual measurements of the professor, how his work compares with that of the others in his classes. Grades, as an evaluation instrument, are also useful to employers in judging the comparative abilities of prospective employees. College presidents and deans also find grades indispensable in the awarding of scholarships and fellowships to worthy students. Again, grades are serviceable in the evaluation of teaching. The competency of a teacher is often disclosed by comparing the grades which he gives with the grades of other professors in similar courses, or by observing the grades which his students make in advance work in his own field of study. Finally, grades have an evaluation function in determining what students lack the interest or ability, or both, to do college work. If there were no grading system of any kind, it would be almost impossible to make regulations for dismissal from college. And without procedures for dismissal in the cases of scholastic failure, many students would continue in college without the least hope of academic happiness or success. Their continuation in college would be unfair to the students themselves, to their families, and to the community at large.

Think of grades and marks as you will, they do remind the student that he lives in a world of competition, a world of ups and downs. A student who completes a program of higher education without facing the rigorous evaluations of a grading system

58

has missed one great chance to learn the helpful lesson that life is full of tests and trials.

18. *Favorable Conditions for Studying*

Arranging a suitable situation for effective studying involves three requirements: (1) *the right mood*, (2) *the right place*, and (3) *the right time*. In recommending procedures for the improvement of learning techniques, I have frequently addressed my remarks to the reader himself rather than to some hypothetical student in the third person singular. The intention was to give directness and pointedness to the suggestions which are submitted.

1. Getting one's self in the right mood for intellectual work calls for two attitudes of mind: (*a*) a definite purpose in studying, and (*b*) attention to the matter at hand.

a. The student can cultivate an aim, or motive, for study in several ways. To begin with, he can define very clearly the task before him by noting the exact nature of the assignment, finding out exactly how much he is supposed to read or write, making certain when the completed work is to be recited or reported. A student cannot be interested in a job before him until he knows accurately and completely what the professor expects him to do. This means that listening carefully to assignments is a very important feature of the class-hour experience.

b. The student can stimulate attention to an academic task by relating the material to be studied to

59

some live project or hobby with which he is concerned, or by attempting to see the importance of the new information for his own personal development, or by connecting the lesson to be studied with knowledge necessary for his later vocational success, or by trying to see the value of the ideas in the book before him for the advancement of society. Another good way to enhance the interest of a subject is to connect it with other studies in the curriculum or with his own fund of knowledge. Few intellectual processes offer more excitement than that of associating new bits of information with the total pattern of one's experience. Again, getting right down to business with a determined purpose to get at the bottom of things is a response which brings very soon the reward of a heightened enthusiasm. Getting below the surface of a passage in literature or science — seeking the causes of the events or doctrines which are being studied or looking for the author's own full meaning — this is the scholar's way to get into the mood for serious intellectual labor. Finally, make your new information a vital part of your immediate experience. Ask questions about it in class, write home about it, discuss it with your roommate, recall it occasionally for your own private analysis, and, above all, enter it correctly and fully in the notebook which you use for recording the material of the course.

2. Selecting a good place is almost as important as getting into the right frame of mind. Often one's study room itself inhibits a satisfactory mood for con-

60

centration. First of all, study, if possible, in a room which is quiet. There are times for your roommate and friends to carry on a noisy " bull-fest " or indulge in a vociferous game of cards, but these diversions are not for study hours. Next, be as comfortable as you can while you study. Dress comfortably, sit comfortably, and have the proper conditions of light, heat, and ventilation. Neither overeat nor skimp on your diet. If you become groggy or begin .to daydream, go out for a walk and breathe in a lot of vitalizing fresh air. Again, arrange your room so the tools of study will be readily accessible. Have your pencils, pen, ink, paper, and blotters within easy reach. Keep close at hand a good dictionary, an English grammar, the high-school texts which you brought with you for review and reference, and the books which you are currently using in your courses. Contrariwise, keep away from the spot sacred for studying the popular magazines and best sellers which entice to pleasant reading when it is time to be bearing down on chemistry, history, or Latin. Psychologists believe that slight distractive sounds are an impetus to energetic concentration. A radio tuned to sweet and low music may stimulate attention; but it is hardly possible to work a problem in calculus or logic and listen at the same time to a blatant orchestra emitting jazz.

3. The matter of conserving time is a problem which every student has to face. Thousands of time budgets have been made by freshmen, but it is very doubtful if a hundred were ever strictly followed. A time

budget should be a student's tool and not his master; it should be the result of careful experimentation and trial in the ordering of his activities and tasks. Experience of many teachers and students has produced, however, a few permanent principles in the employment of study time. First of all, it is advisable for the student to keep regular hours for the preparation of his various subjects. He thereby gets the habit of studying certain courses at certain times, and habit is always a saver of energy and effort. Another good practice is to rotate the courses one studies during the day. Changing now and then from one type of subject to another prevents monotony and boredom, and permits periodically a freshness of approach. The time allotment on any one course varies with different students, but it is safe to say that no course should be given more than two hours' study at a sitting. It is also a good idea to use the period between different subjects for diversion — a walk across the campus, a program on the radio, a cup of coffee, or a telephone conversation with a congenial person. A student must budget his time to give his class periods and study hours first place, but he must take into consideration the many other legitimate interests of campus life. If the statistical studies carried on in my own college are representative of the situation generally, the satisfactory American student averages about twenty-one hours a week in the preparation of his lessons. This leaves him a generous amount of time for extra-curricular activities — social engagements, amusements, lectures, concerts, church, fraternity or

62

sorority affairs, and many other events. These activities, as we shall observe in a later discussion, play an important part in the development of a complete personality.

I have not said anything regarding the time budget of the student who must work his way through college. He naturally cannot devote as much time to recreation and extra-curricular activities as his classmate who is sufficiently supplied with funds. The employed student, however, can have the assurance that he is developing attitudes and skills in his job which eventually may be a great deal more beneficial than experiences on a track team or in a class play. The student who carries a job while going to college needs to be certain that a regular schedule of classes, taken along with his outside employment, does not result in academic failure or ill health. The average student can work four or five hours a day and still make satisfactory grades, but the fact remains that he might get much more out of his courses if he were not limited in his study time. The employed student should examine carefully the educational and physiological advantages of a light program of scholastic work. It might take him a few months longer to graduate, but the increased richness of his academic experience would be ample compensation.

63

19. *Reading for Pleasure and Profit*

Since practically all of the studying and learning processes depend mainly upon reading, this activity is probably the most important of all the techniques of liberal education. Reading occurs so naturally and easily in adult experience that we forget that there are certain prerequisites to its effective employment. Below are some of the practical procedures which increase the speed and efficacy of reading. They require no physical examination or treatment of the eyes, and any student can use them.

Before you get down to the serious business of reading a book for study purposes, you should make some preliminary preparations. First of all, you should acquire, if possible, some information concerning the author. *Who's Who in America* or some other biographical directory may have a brief history of the author's life. It will be interesting to find out what the writer's main interests and achievements have been, and what other books he has published. You will then enter into the book with a certain feeling of familiarity and confidence. A second thing to do is to examine carefully the preface of the book. This will usually give you some idea of the background, aim, and organization of the work. You will thereby acquire a more definite plan for your own approach to it. A third suggestion by way of preliminary attack is to skim through the whole book before concentrating on any of its pages. Glancing at the table of contents, noting titles of divisions and subdivisions, and scanning chapter summaries will help you to get the "hang" of the book; you will proceed through it with a sense of direction and a feeling of expectancy. If this hasty survey discloses any points or passages which seem to be unusually important, make a note of them for special attention when you reach them later in your thorough study of the book.

When the preliminary steps have been taken, you are ready for careful reading and study. I suggest that your reading will be more thorough and intelligent if you do three things as you read: (1) *concentrate*, (2) *correlate*, and (3) *criticize*. Let us examine each of these suggestions.

1. Concentration in reading not only demands all the aids to attention which were indicated in our examination of study habits but calls for two special types of response. In the first place, you will have to take the time and trouble to learn the meanings of the words and sentences which are used if you are to be able to keep your mind on a book. It is impossible to hold your attention long and intensely upon printed material which conveys a sense of ambiguity or is lacking in meaning. Form the habit of using a dictionary when you read. The failure to know the definition of a term in a textbook may cause misunderstanding of an entire theory, and even in the reading of fiction the point of a whole plot may be lost because a word or phrase is not understood. It is so tempting to pass by foreign language expressions

65

without looking up their correct translation, and it is so easy to skip tables and graphs which, if carefully examined, would clarify and demonstrate an entire argument or thesis. It is safe to say that one major difference between a good and a poor student lies in the unwillingness of the former to let vague terminology pass by without clarification.

The second condition of effective concentration in reading is the capacity to read rapidly. The slow reader finds it difficult to concentrate because the whole process becomes monotonous and fatigue sets in. If you would do as well as the average reader, you should read ordinary reading matter at the rate of about two hundred and twenty-five words a minute. Rapid reading depends upon two factors: eye efficiency and alertness of mind. Defective vision requires the treatment of a physician or oculist; the latter condition is one that you yourself can cultivate and improve. Speed in reading requires mental alertness because it means quick apprehension of the ideas in a passage, and not merely perceptional awareness of the particular words. Words are symbols and tools and should be respected only as such. The mind of the reader should leap instantaneously beyond the word to its meaning, and beyond a group of words to their total significance. Earnest and continuous diligence in reading for ideas rather than signs will soon enable one to comprehend at one glance the meaning of a clause or sentence, or even of a paragraph. I am, of course, not affirming that reading must in every instance be of this generalized, reflective sort. Often it is very necessary to attend to an item as a specific and separate topic. Quotations, numerical summaries, dates, directions, rules, and regulations are a few of the cases which frequently must be treated in reading as significant in and for themselves alone.

Reading for ideas calls for the development of one's intellectual capacity. The effective reader must have a broad and systematic background of experience in order that he may quickly discern, on the basis of similar responses in the past, the meanings which the printed words convey. This means, of course, that to become a good and speedy reader one must read, and read, and read. The more you read, the better you read — that is, if you are a reader who thinks as he looks. Cultivating the habit of reading reflectively increases the reader's capacity to discriminate the more important from the less important ideas. The power of discrimination, in turn, speeds up reading because it prevents undue attention to minor details. The secret of fast and proficient reading is to find as soon as possible the primary and fundamental conceptions of the author.

When you are just commencing the habit of rapid reading, you will probably miss many of the important meanings of a chapter or a book. In the beginning, therefore, retrace your steps by going over the passages in a more concentrated, cautious way. Compare the number of the significant ideas obtained by both methods. Carry on this experiment again and again with various kinds of reading material. You will soon find yourself a reader of meanings and not a mere looker at words.

2. From the role of concentration in reading let us pass to the function of correlation. By correlation here I mean the process of connecting the ideas of the author with your own life or with the world at large. Only in this way will the subject matter of the book become vital or useful to you. Integrate the views presented with those of other writers and scholars in the same field of knowledge. Relate them to some social or scientific problem, and try to discover whether they have any practical significance for human affairs. Think of them historically, and try to evaluate them as representing progress or retrogression in the movement of culture. And to ascertain whether or not the ideas of the book have become a part of your own complex of knowledge, recall and recite them to yourself. Even construct some questions on the material of the book and see whether or not you can pass your own examination.

3. The third process in proficient reading is criticism. Form your own critical opinions of the book you are reading. Evaluate its style, sincerity, clarity, consistency, validity, and interest. Ask yourself questions like these: Does the author have facts and evidence to support his arguments and conclusions? Has he given all the facts in the support of this theory? Has he been fair to opposing doctrines? Read the reviews of authoritative critics and see whether or not their opinions coincide with your own. If somebody

asks you about the book, you will be able to give a candid estimate of its worth. And, what is more important, you will know how significant a place to give to the author's ideas in your own scheme of thought.

Criticism cannot be completely separated from correlation in one's response to a book. In fact, criticism and correlation are aspects of one intellectual process, and that is the process of *understanding*. The understanding of a book may not be complete or just, — it may fall far short of an authoritative interpretation, — but it is the thing which gives a book life in a reader's mind. Wisdom is the desire to profit by another man's knowledge; understanding makes the other man's knowledge your very own. Get wisdom, but also get understanding, the ancient proverb profoundly advised.

In concluding my discussion of reading, I wish to suggest a procedure for assimilating effectively the oral material of classroom lectures. Except for the physiological differences between hearing and sight, learning by listening and learning by looking are very much the same. The principles which apply in the successful response to a professor's spoken words are fundamentally like those which pertain to the proficient reading of an author's book. The listener, like the reader, must be on the lookout for ideas and not for words. Like the good reader, the good listener must be discriminating in his reactions; he must respond with thought and not merely with sense; he must correlate the ideas received with those of his wider experience; and he must seek to remember what he hears. Whether words are written or spoken, they need definition, interpretation, application, and retention. If a student can perform these four processes in regard to what he sees and to what he hears, he can take any academic examination without flurry or fear.

Remembering, as indicated briefly in the paragraph above, is a necessary and important activity in the intellectual process. I have already emphasized the significance, in learning, of ideas retained in memory. Forgetfulness is the thief of the scholastic world, the student's Enemy Number One. The principles for the retention of ideas are very similar to those which underlie the acquisition of ideas. In the first place, you cannot remember clearly what you did not originally learn with distinctness. Vague and undefined ideas are soon forgotten. In the second place, ideas to be remembered must be located in some chain of thought. Ideas which have no logical relationship to other ideas are very difficult to recall. If you wish to guarantee an idea a permanent and accessible place in your memory, associate it by cause or effect, resemblance or difference, or some other relationship, with ideas already secure in your mind. In the third place, memorizing, like reading, must be practiced repeatedly. If you have to memorize a passage of poetry or prose, say it over and over, write it and rewrite it, think it again and again. This does not mean, however, that you should memorize the material in one period. Only the very best students can profitably spend more than fifteen minutes of memo-

rizing at one sitting. Distribute your memorizing
exercises over an expanse of time, using the intervals
for other types of activity. Do not be afraid of memorizing too hard. We are usually tempted to cease the
process of memorization after the first instance of recall. If you wish to be sure that you will be able to
recollect some certain material at a later date, *over-
learn* that material now.

20. *Extra-curricular Attractions*

No examination of a student's scholastic program
can be complete without reference to the influence of
the extra-curricular activities. The events and activities in which a student participates outside of the
classroom, library, and laboratory are highly important in his social and educational development.
Athletics, dramatics, musical groups, campus publica-
tions, student government, religious societies, and the
many other forms of organized extra-curricular response
have direct effect on his academic attitudes and aims.

Several values of extra-curricular activities are
worthy of mention. In the first place, the student
who engages in a reasonable number of nonscholastic
events on the campus is freed from any morbid
tendency to exaggerate his own troubles or prejudices.
He is prevented from cultivating an " inferiority complex," or feeling of self-debasement, which makes
him shy and inadequate in social adjustments. The
student who enjoys a wholesome extra-curricular experience does not have to develop irregular and

71

extravagant types of behavior to convince himself and others of his personal adequacy. He does not have to show by immorality or cynical snobbishness that he is as good as the next one. His participation with his college mates in the various student activities of the campus automatically reveals his normal and agreeable character.

In the second place, extra-curricular activities enable the student to enjoy the companionship and influence of many types of people. Ordinarily athletics, dramatics, and the other campus affairs are open to students on a democratic basis, and students of every financial condition, social status, cultural background, race, and religion are allowed to participate. If extra-curricular activities are free from campus politics, they help students to transcend the exclusiveness of fraternity and sorority connections. Again, in the experiences of extra-curricular programs the student can learn to appreciate the interests and purposes of the opposite sex. No better way is available for the young men and young women of the campus to associate together than in the co-operative enterprises of a co-ed extra-curricular activity. Moreover, in extra-curricular activities the students can enjoy fellowship with professors in congenial and informal manner. Often a professor's most effective influence is expressed in his services as adviser to a campus organization — there he is " just one of the bunch." Finally, in extra-curricular affairs the student frequently meets men and women of the community who are leaders in the world of practical affairs. His religious activities

72

bring him in contact with local ministers, his journalistic endeavors take him to the offices of newspapermen, his dramatic interests bring him opportunities to associate with the visiting actors, and so on. These relationships are only occasional and temporary; but they give the student a chance to face some actual problems of societal living, and not infrequently they lead to connections which mean vocational placement when college days are over.

Often the extra-curricular experiences bring delights which continue long after graduation. The devotion to a college or university which is known as alumni spirit cannot be adequately generated in the classroom or laboratory. It grows in the atmosphere of free and jolly comradeship — an atmosphere much more prevalent in the locker room of a gymnasium or the editorial office of the campus newspaper than in the research stacks of a library. Again, in extra-curricular activities students often develop interests and hobbies which last for a lifetime. The delights of swimming, tennis, painting, singing, and other activities of an exciting life are very frequently the continuation of pleasures appreciated first in an amateur college performance. And, last of all, the most permanent friendships of college life are those between the fellows on the same football squad, colleagues on the same debating team, or actors in the same commencement show. A student will soon forget who sat next to him in freshman mathematics or advanced history, but he will long remember the fellow who played next to him on the football team,

73

or the girl who acted opposite to him in the annual college play.

There are a few warnings, however, which must be given regarding extra-curricular activities. They are, after all, the " side show." Students come to college to study, and not to play. The participant must be very careful that his extra-curricular activities are not too numerous; he cannot afford to let them interfere with his homework. Moreover, he must watch his health; it does not pay to become a B.M.O.C., a " big man on the campus," if this achievement brings on a nervous breakdown or a permanent illness. Finally, the student must not allow success in the extra-curricular area to go to his head. There is no place on a college campus for a braggart or a bully. The gate to extra-curricular achievement and pleasure never opens widely to the snob.

21. *The Principles of Intellectual Fellowship*

Any discussion of the techniques of liberal education should consider the community aspects of college life. The student is a member of a very compact and closely knit social unit. Like the family, state, lodge, labor union, and other groups in modern society, the college represents the desire of human beings to unite together in a common fellowship to achieve a common goal. Moreover, the college community represents the highest social idealism of man and requires the finest type of social customs. Both in its spirit and in

74

its method the college community is an ideal for all other human associations. As a fellowship of teachers and learners dedicated to the discovery and spread of truth, it is social organization at its best. Like the church, the college is a spiritual society, and only those with lofty aspiration and sincere good will can ever truly belong.

To indicate in what respects the college may be regarded as a community and to indicate the principles to which its members must be loyal, I refer you to some verses in the New Testament. Whether you are a Catholic, Protestant, Christian Scientist, or Hindu, these Scriptural sentences will bring you six distinct features of the ideal college fellowship. Here are the Biblical assertions which present the standards of academic social life: " And Jesus said to the Jews who believed in him: 'If you continue in my word, you shall be my disciples and you shall know the truth, and the truth shall make you free. And if the Son shall make you free, you shall be free indeed.'" Let us examine separately the educational ideals in this significant pronouncement of the master teacher and friend.

The first necessity in an educational community is *confidence in teachers*. " And Jesus said unto the Jews who *believed in him...*" No college student can receive intellectual benefit from a professor to whom he does not look with affection and esteem. The history of America's great institutions of higher learning can be reduced almost entirely to the biography of their most beloved teachers. One of the most frequent and tragic

75

mistakes of freshmen is to judge a college instructor by superficial standards. Often first-year students will fail completely to appreciate the profound scholarship of a teacher because they pay more attention to his manners, looks, or clothes than they do to his ideas.

The second principle of the ideal college community is *fidelity to the laws of learning* — " If you *continue in my word* . . ." Success in scholarship, like attainment in music, art, athletics, or any other pursuit, means strict obedience to the rules of the game. There are laws of thinking which are just as rigorous and inevitable as the laws of chemical reaction or the laws of falling bodies. Only strict adherence to these principles will prevent the partiality and falsity which characterize the thoughts of a careless student. Correct and efficient learning, however, requires more than a knowledge of the rules of attention, observation, memory, and reason; it means persistence and diligence in conformity to the rules of learning. " If ye continue in my word . . .," warns the great teacher; continual and constant diligence in learning is the price of intellectual leadership and success.

The third requirement is *comradeship with fellow students* — " You shall be my *disciples*." There is no finer or more lasting friendship than that which comes when several individuals are loyal to a common idea or program. In college halls this type of friendship primarily centers around the loyalty of a group of students to a professor with a new social or scientific theory. The exhilarating experience of association

76

with fellow students who enjoy together the inspirational influence of a truly scholarly teacher is one of the supreme privileges of college life. For many youths the exhilaration of discipleship is known for the first time in loyalty, with others, to the ideals and discoveries of an intellectual pioneer. The lessons of discipleship are desperately needed today. We need millions of men and women who can appreciate the fact that followers are just as important in a democracy as leaders. Liberty does not mean the repudiation of leadership. It means rational and co-operative understanding of the ideas which guide the leader. An ordinary citizen who accepts with appreciation and intelligence the laws drawn up by governmental authorities is not a slave or a tool. He is a free man, because he knows that his actions follow the principles of reason. There can be no higher type of personal liberty than the right to obey the commands of a rational will, whether that will is one's own or the will of a nation. This is the principle of free discipleship, and calls upon the citizen to be everlastingly certain that his will and that of his governing society manifest the benevolence and justice which come with sound rational insight. Liberal education is not merely a prerogative of leaders who need intelligence to govern well; it is the privilege of the average citizen, who has the right to know whether or not his leaders are faithful to their trust.

The fourth principle is the *discrimination of the truth* — "And you shall *know the truth.*" Knowledge of the truth is more than understanding true ideas.

77

Truth for truth's sake is only one function of truth. There is also truth for religion's sake, for government's sake, for art's sake, and for all the other interests of human living. To know truth fundamentally is to know its meaning for life — to know how ideas help man to realize to the full the potentialities of the human spirit. Truth is more than a system of ideas. It tells us more than that ideas are clear, useful, and consistent. Truth is the quality of the man who holds the right ideas. It is the principle of sincerity and integrity in a person's moral being. Truth that does not organize and vitalize one's entire outlook and character is truth only in name. The truth which sets a person free is more than a pattern of words. It is the essence of a person integrated and impelled by an all-inclusive and all-important life ideal. Truth that is really truth is not knowledge removed from life; it is knowledge made flesh, dwelling in the very lives of men and women.

The fifth principle of an intellectual community follows immediately from the fourth, as we have just seen; it is *the appreciation of intellectual freedom* — "*And the truth shall make you free.*" There are many kinds of freedom — such as freedom from poverty, pain, or tyranny. The freedom which comes with the attainment of truth is an achievement of the mind — it is escape from fear, ignorance, boredom, hate, and the other foes of the peaceful and orderly mind. Only with this kind of liberty can man enjoy the aesthetic experiences of art, music, and religion, or formulate practical ways of meeting the problems of everyday living. This freedom is so important because it is man's best way to realize, in his own innermost being, that he is an individual, valuable on his own account, and worthy to enjoy the noblest experiences of the human spirit. Whatever his station or occupation in life, he knows that, when he lives in the world of art, literature, science, philosophy, religion, or music, he transcends the realm of space and time. However successful a person may be in the world of practical affairs, if he cannot sincerely contemplate the ideals of truth, goodness, and beauty, he cannot know the truth that really makes man free.

The sixth and last principle of an effective college community is *appreciation of moral excellence* — " *And if the Son shall make you free, you shall be free indeed.*" *Son* here refers, of course, to Jesus. Whatever you think of him as a religious leader, you will have to admit that he has ever been in Western thought the model of personal ethical perfection. Neither intellectual superiority nor financial independence nor political influence can bring one personal success without a foundation of righteous thought and conduct. There is a freedom of the heart as well as a freedom of the mind, and this freedom of the heart is the exuberance and power which come to an individual when he follows the paths of purity, honesty, and good will. An undergraduate can follow all the rules of effective study and meet all the curricular requirements of his college, but if he does not obey the principles of social morality he can never become a respected or dependable person. To live in a com-

79

munity successfully one must treat the other members of the community with honor and esteem. He must treat his fellows as ends in themselves, and not as means to his own self-interest. The student who cannot respect himself cannot appreciate the dignity of other persons. If liberal education is to be conducive to sound social ethics, it must convince youth that only unselfish and right-minded people can treat their associates with fairness and respect. The college community and democratic society as a whole can enjoy peace and order only when their members have the moral idealism to treat one another as free and responsible persons.

So much for our discussion of the rules and circumstances of learning. We are now ready to survey the various courses which constitute the academic curriculum. The college student must know not only *how* but *what* to study.

THE ART
OF SELF-DEVELOPMENT

CURRICULA
OF LIBERAL EDUCATION

THE COURSES of study are the most essential feature of the college experience. They provide the stuff of a liberal education. They furnish the substance out of which lawyers, doctors, ministers, teachers, engineers, and all college graduates mold the ideas which control and govern their lives. There are many kinds of curricula, with many types of purpose, but they are all alike in offering material for the student mind. The best criterion for the measurement of academic achievement is a student's comprehension of curricular subject matter. The more a student learns, understands, and remembers, the better he will be as a thinker. In a college education there is no adequate substitute for the ideas received in lecture, library, conference, or research.

22. *The Educational Import of the Curriculum*

The curricular feature of academic life is so significant that colleges are often classified on the basis of their courses of study.

1. The college of the *strictly cultural* tradition is limited in the number of its studies; it retains the classical languages and higher mathematics in its required offerings; it avoids the so-called fads and frills in educational theory; it places more responsibility upon the individual student than upon official coun-

seling services in the development of intellectual efficacy; it definitely designs its program for prospective leaders in the learned professions — in short, this type of college continues the ideal of an aristocratic education for the " gentleman and the scholar."

2. A second type of college presents a more *individualized* program of studies. An exponent of the methods and aims of " progressive education, " it allows the student a wider choice of courses and a more liberal schedule of electives. It encourages the student to arrange his curriculum on the basis of interests or projects which are of great concern to him. The unity of the studies is not derived from any traditional and standardized pattern fixed by the conventional professional mind. The order and coherence in the student's courses of study is the product of his own reflection and purpose, and the unifying principle may be changed when new problems, demanding new organizations of thinking, arise. This " progressive " form of college education is directed to prospective workers in all walks of life, and attempts seriously to provide a social training which will prepare its graduates, whatever their vocations, for cooperative and democratic living.

3. A third type of collegiate program deplores the intellectual relativism and the moral skepticism of the contemporary American outlook. It emphasizes the necessity of courses which disclose the permanent and universal aspects of human culture. It claims that education should be devoted to the study of the major

works of the world's greatest minds. Its objective is similar to that of the aristocratic tradition, but it is more concerned with an analysis of the fundamental concepts of the arts and the sciences. If it has a social purpose, this purpose is based on the belief that only in a search for ultimate principles can students really learn to think. And thinking, this theory insistently maintains, is the only remedy for our modern societal ills. Colleges which support this doctrine of education usually stress either metaphysics or theology as the basic discipline in the quest for authoritative understanding. For the lack of a better term, the adjective *scholastic* may be appropriately applied to this kind of college education. For its purpose, in principle, is that of the scholasticism of medieval culture.

4. A fourth type of institution of higher learning, frequently called the *general* college, frankly plans its curricular offerings so as to provide guidance and inspiration for everyday living. Its courses usually require no intellectual background other than that furnished by the high school, and they are not intended to serve as prerequisites for advanced specialized or professional curricula. The main purpose of this kind of education is to provide information of broad human interest and immediate practical value. Many of the courses in the curriculum are of the orientation and survey type. The program followed usually includes a great deal of individualized personnel service and vocational guidance. The value of the natural and social sciences for civilized life is discussed, and in the

85

humanities suggestions for the enjoyment of art, literature, and music are offered. The curriculum of the " general " college, usually designed for two years of work, is, in a word, a preparation for well-informed and responsible citizenship. It can be recommended to all students who lack either the interest, money, or ability to take the advanced, specialized courses of a college or university.

5. For a fifth type of college, I suggest one which combines the best curricular features of the four types just described. The ideal four-year college of liberal arts would be one which in the first two years would incorporate in its program the most satisfactory aspects of " general " and " progressive " education, and which in its last two years would plan its work according to the objectives of the " aristocratic " and "scholastic" traditions. Admitting enthusiastically that the liberal college must provide ample personnel and guidance services and admitting also that these services should be conducted to meet the peculiar needs of individual students, I contend that the curriculum of the four-year college, in the main, should not serve the interest of any group or career. Freely allowing for elective courses on the basis of individual abilities and preferences, the program of study of an arts college should result in a unified, total experience, equally significant for lawyer, teacher, housewife, or farmer. There is a place and need for certain offerings which furnish useful information for effective personal and vocational life, but an education worthy of the B.A.

degree should produce, in line with its broadest purpose, a quality of mind more fundamental and universal than any immediately practical outlook. This basic and inclusive cultural perspective cannot be attained in any short-cut course. It requires maturity of judgment and depth of understanding. An appreciation of the enduring meanings of physical and human nature is not achieved by quickly learning what others have said and written about man and his world. The arts college is a place to " see life steadily and to see it whole," and this is an attainment which cannot be hurried. If students would only realize the importance of this principle in the development of effective personality, they would not be in such a rush to get through college. The wise student will be patient and persistent enough to let the college get through him.

The next several sections describe separately the curriculum of the typical liberal college. The discussions are designed to help the student in the choice of studies for his own academic program. The main contents, methods, and values of each course are outlined, and the interrelations between the different fields of knowledge are indicated. The reader will realize that the division of the curriculum into different courses is an arbitrary procedure, fundamentally untrue to the unity of human knowledge. Science and culture know no boundaries. The lines of separation between the various disciplines and studies are artificial devices, set up to enable us to concentrate for practical purposes on certain sections of our total experience. There has been no attempt to include all of the courses and curricula presented in colleges of liberal arts. I have included only those essential courses of study which are offered in the standard program of higher education. There are no special sections on English composition, speech, and dramatics. I have tried to make the discussion of literature inclusive enough to indicate the fundamental features of all the language arts. In presenting courses of study as ways of self-development in college, I also wish to emphasize the fact that college courses, when adequately taught and studied, become the basis for intellectual growth through one's entire life.

I have commenced my survey of the various courses with statements concerning mathematics, the foundation subject of all the sciences. After mathematics the remaining courses in the college curriculum are discussed under four main headings: the Physical Sciences, the Biological Sciences, the Social Sciences, and the Humanities.

23. *Mathematics — the Master Science*

Mathematics differs from all other branches of science in the important respect that it does not use as its subject matter the content of any other field of knowledge. It does not borrow from other areas in the way psychology secures data from biology, or biology from chemistry. Mathematics is independent of other branches of learning, and must be defined in

88

terms of its own content and method. The forms of mathematics usually apply to objects in the natural order, and frequently mathematical concepts are derived in the observation of actual events; but the validity of mathematics is not measured by its relevancy to things which we perceive. The truth of mathematics is formal rather than material in its meaning, and is evaluated in terms of its own inner consistency and its fidelity to its own fundamental axioms and postulates. The realm of mathematics transcends the domain of sensory experience — it is a mental world created by the abstracting and universalizing powers of the human mind. Mathematics deals with pure quantities, numbers, and relations. When it deals with space, it describes it in terms of conceptual, abstract, ideal space. It uses the method of induction in that it does make generalizations and constructions; but in the main it follows closely the method of rigorous deductive logic, arriving at conclusions which are justified entirely by premises postulated at the outset.

Mathematics may be divided into three main divisions: (1) *algebra*, (2) *geometry*, and (3) *analysis*.

1. Algebra is the branch of mathematics which represents the properties and relations of numbers by using, as general symbols, the letters of the alphabet. Using also a system of signs for the various operations which are carried on, it transforms what would be a very complicated arithmetical problem into a fairly simple procedure.

89

2. Geometry deals with the properties of space. Assuming certain fundamental characters of space, called axioms, the geometer derives certain conclusions about space from the nature and relations of the points, lines, curves, surfaces, and solids which constitute a spatial entity. Geometry is of several kinds: *Euclidean geometry*, which discusses the three-dimensional spaces of ordinary experience; *non-Euclidean geometry*, which employs axioms which transcend the space of common-sense experience; *analytic geometry*, which employs algebraic equations in the description of geometrical figures and relations; and *projective geometry*, an inclusive geometry that includes discussions of both Euclidean and non-Euclidean spatial forms.

3. Analysis embraces the two areas of mathematics which a student will enter when he takes *calculus* and *differential equations*. In addition to algebra, geometry, and analysis, mathematics also includes two well-known features: *arithmetic*, the science of numbers as applied mainly in computations, and *trigonometry*, the science which enables one to measure triangles in the most simple and expeditious way.

As an organized form of knowledge, with definite principles and uses, mathematics dates back at least forty centuries. The Babylonians and the Egyptians were the first to employ highly developed number systems and theories of geometry, although anthropologists have reason to believe that counting, with a base of ten (the number of fingers on both hands), was carried on by primitive peoples before the dawn of civilization or recorded history. The Greeks were the first to develop mathematics as a science, and some of the early Greek philosophers extended mathematics beyond its practical applications into the areas of profound metaphysical speculation. Pythagoras (sixth century B.C.) and Plato (427–347 B.C.) interpreted the ultimate nature of the universe in terms of mathematical principles. The greatest figure in Greek mathematics was Euclid, who lived about 300 B.C. Euclid's employment of geometric forms in the reasoning process influenced the entire development of mathematical theory. Other important Greek mathematicians, both of the third century B.C., were Archimedes and Apollonius. The Romans, concerned mainly with applied arithmetic, devised what is commonly known as the Roman system of numerals. The Arabians kept mathematics alive during the Middle Ages, conserving, in particular, the decimal system introduced by the Hindus. In the seventeenth century in western Europe mathematics was developed by such scholars and scientists as René Descartes (1596–1650), the inventor of analytic geometry; Isaac Newton (1642–1727), the great synthesizer of mathematical principles; and Gottfried Wilhelm Leibnitz (1646–1716), the inventor of the differential calculus. During the eighteenth and nineteenth centuries mathematics advanced through the formulation of the theories of function, probability, error, non-Euclidean geometry, and symbolic logic. During the past few decades the chief service of mathematics has been its

91

development of the principles which permitted the formulation of the concept of relativity in physics and the new atomism of chemistry.

The values of mathematics for the clearer understanding and the more effective manipulation of natural and human events are inestimable. In the first place, higher mathematics offers a pattern for philosophical speculations about the fundamental meaning of things. The notion of logical order in the universe, as portrayed in Platonism, Stoicism, and pantheism, was the result of a mathematical model in metaphysics. The mechanistic interpretation of the cosmos, which prevailed from the seventeenth to the twentieth century, reflected a mathematical conception of the interrelations between events. Again, the idea of purpose in natural phenomena indicates the influence of statistical correlation on philosophy. Finally, the sweep of mathematics into imaginary realms, the universality of its application, the aesthetic appeal of its orderliness and accuracy, and the permanence of its postulates — all are very attractive and encouraging to the philosophical mind.

I need not emphasize the practical and technical values of mathematics. As a subject in the curriculum it is a discipline which develops the needed art of rigorous, precise, and sustained thinking. Physics, astronomy, chemistry, and engineering are inconceivable without the bases of mathematical knowledge. Neither business nor economics could continue without the employment of mathematical devices. Finance, insurance, marketing, banking, and other processes of the commercial world could not continue without the use of numbers and numerical calculations. And when one considers the social values of statistics, he realizes that the services of governmental bureaus, the investigations in agriculture, social service, and public health, and the findings of psychological and educational research would all be impossible without the fundamental theories of mathematics.

Among vocational opportunities in mathematics the following appear to be most promising: teaching mathematics in high school, college, or professional school; statistical or actuarial positions with large business organizations, insurance companies, or governmental agencies; research positions in physics, chemistry, bacteriology, genetics, medicine, and engineering. A college graduate, whether he goes into mathematics professionally or not, will find mathematical knowledge very valuable not only as an occasional aid in his vocational work but also as a useful instrument in the efficient management of home affairs.

24. *The World of the Physical Sciences*

In the college curriculum the following four physical sciences are usually offered: (1) *astronomy*, (2) *physics*, (3) *chemistry*, and (4) *geology*. They are all alike in that they seek to describe and explain the natural phenomena in man's external environment; and they all depend mainly on the inductive method

93

THE ART OF SELF-DEVELOPMENT

of scientific investigation, that is, on the method of passing progressively through the stages of observation, hypothesis, theory, and law. Each of these sciences starts with immediate specific, factual data and moves through tentative and partial verification to the widest possible generalizations. Like all science, the physical sciences are concerned with the explanation of events in terms of their causes and their effects. They are particularly significant in the curriculum in . that they introduce the student to the most exacting type of research work and to the accurate use of very delicate laboratory instruments. Let us notice some of the main features in each of these four fields.

1. ASTRONOMY

Astronomy deals with the motions, nature, interrelationships, and evolution of stars, planets, and other heavenly bodies, with special attention to their relation to our earth. The subject is divided into these areas: *celestial mechanics*, the study of the heavenly bodies as influenced by gravitation; *astrometry*, the study of the positions and dimensions of the celestial bodies; and *astrophysics*, the study of the physical and chemical nature of astronomical bodies as revealed by the spectroscope.

Until modern times the ancient theory of Ptolemy, presented in the second century A.D., held sway in astronomy. This was the theory that the earth was the central body around which the sun and planets

94

revolved. In the sixteenth century Nicholas Copernicus (1473–1543) offered the new theory that the earth and planets revolve about the sun. Johannes Kepler (1571–1630) showed that the path of the planets about the sun is not a circle but an ellipse. Galileo (1564–1642), inventing and using the telescope, discovered spots on the sun and thereby refuted the ancient belief that the heavenly bodies are perfect. In the seventeenth century Isaac Newton (1642–1727) combined the investigations of Copernicus, Kepler, Galileo, and others into a colossal mathematical system under the law of universal gravitation. During the nineteenth century, astronomers were able with the aid of the spectroscope to determine the composition of the stars and the various rates of their motions. The twentieth century has seen a great modification in astronomy in the development of the theory of four-dimensional space-time as a revision of the old tridimensional view of space. The new view is a part of the recent revolutionary conception of relativity.

The value of astronomy for liberal education is reflected most of all in the new ideas of spatial magnitude which it has brought into the human imagination. Our universe has been enlarged thousands and thousands of times by the use of the mighty telescopes of the present day. The astronomer has given us detailed information concerning millions of stars, or suns, many of which are hundreds of times larger than our own sun. And he has told us about thousands of spiral nebulae so far away in space that the light from them takes more than a million years to reach us. The one-hundred-inch Hooker telescope on Mt. Wilson, California, takes in about sixteen thousand times as much light as the eye. And now a telescope is being completed at the California Institute of Technology with a two-hundred-inch reflector and with the power to carry human vision four times as far as the Hooker telescope. No subject in the curriculum can offer more fascination or mystical satisfaction than astronomy, with its marvelous disclosures regarding the birth, life, and death of the stars. Light is thrown upon the questions of religion and philosophy concerning the origin of life, the beginning of time, and the evolution of nature by many of the pronouncements of astronomy.

From the standpoint of vocational placement the only opportunities available are in the teaching of astronomy in college or university, directing observatories, operating telescopes, research in connection with the larger observatories and weather bureaus, popular lecturing, and administrative work in a planetarium. It is fair to say that astronomy is a very restricted field, and offers very few openings for a professional career.

2. PHYSICS

Physics deals with the properties of nonliving things which are fundamental to all of these things and which are independent of chemical constitution or change. The molecular structure of the atom, for instance, is

96

a problem for research in physics. In each of its considerations physics is concerned with the forms, effects, and transformations of the energy involved in the situation being studied. The science of physics has the following areas of investigation: (*a*) *mechanics*, the study of forces and their effects in the production of rest or motion in bodies; (*b*) *heat*, the study of the motions of molecules as affected by temperature; (*c*) *electricity and magnetism;* (*d*) *sound;* (*e*) *light;* and (*f*) *properties of matter and the structure of the atom.*

The first great physicist was Archimedes, a Greek of the third century B.C., who worked out laws for the displacement of bodies in water and for the use of the lever. Galileo and Newton, already mentioned as astronomers, were also great physicists, especially in their studies regarding the laws of motion. In the nineteenth century Joule (1818–1889) showed that heat is a form of energy; Michael Faraday (1791–1867) and Clerk-Maxwell discovered and developed electromagnetism; in 1881 the Michelson-Morley experiment, which refuted the ether theory, was conducted; and in 1895 Röntgen discovered X rays. In the last few years great work has been done on the radioactivity of the atom, and the theory of relativity has changed the absolute conceptions of time, space, length, and mass propounded in the Newtonian conception of the physical world. The reality of the new physics is not a matter of definite qualitative, tridimensional character but of energy wave forms in a four-dimensional space-time.

97

Like astronomy, physics has a philosophical importance. It sheds a great deal of light on the ancient philosophical problems regarding the nature of matter, force, motion, time, and space. Its laws and principles, like those of mathematics and astronomy, also provide a logical background for the construction of views of the cosmos and of ultimate reality. For example, the principle of indeterminacy in recent physics has had a great influence on the philosopher's ideas of natural law and human freedom. For a training in strict, accurate scientific thinking no discipline is more profitable than the successful completion of a course in laboratory physics. The practical values of physics are countless. The inventions in matters of lighting, transportation, communication, engineering, and in a host of other lines are all the result of applied physical principles. Telephones, radios, television, motion pictures, color photography, automobiles, airplanes, ultraviolet lamps, artificial refrigeration, and airconditioning are but a few of the instruments and conveniences of civilization which have resulted from productive research in physics.

Positions in physics or in occupations based on competency in physics are available in many fields: teaching in high school, college, and university; research professorships; research for governmental bureaus, foundations, industry, and business; and the sales of electrical and other appliances. The Army, Navy, and Air Corps also require experts with a background in physics. Physics also provides the basic training for work in optometry, or applied optics.

Finally, elementary knowledge of physics is very useful in a trade or in doing the everyday tasks which require mechanical information and craftsmanship.

3. CHEMISTRY

Chemistry is the study, in qualitative and quantitative terms, of the changes which occur in the composition of material bodies. The causes, energy transformations, and laws of these changes are systematically investigated. Chemistry is divided into the following areas of work: (*a*) *general chemistry*, the basic study of the chemical elements, their nature and combinations; (*b*) *analytical chemistry*, the testing of chemical substances to determine the quality or quantity of the elements of which they consist; (*c*) *organic chemistry*, the study of the compounds of carbon; (*d*) *inorganic chemistry*, the study of noncarbon compounds; and (*e*) *physical chemistry*, the study of the ultimate physical or mathematical nature of chemical substances.

Alchemy was the predecessor of the science of chemistry. It began in the ancient theory that all matter is composed of the same stuff and that all metals, in particular, can be changed into one basic metal. The ancient Alexandrian alchemists actually tried to change the baser metals into gold. The medieval alchemists applied the same principle when they tried to find a single cure for all human ills. Another notion which persisted from early Greek thought was the idea that all materials can be reduced to four substances (fire, air, earth, and water) or to combinations of these substances. Continuing through the Middle Ages was the belief that the various elements in nature combined because of a certain affinity they had for each other. As late as the seventeenth century, combustion was explained by the phlogiston theory; phlogiston was thought to be a mysterious substance which, in escaping from substances, caused combustion to occur. In the seventeenth century Robert Boyle (1627–1691) presented the idea that the elements of bodies are atoms of different shapes and sizes, and in the eighteenth century Antoine Lavoisier (1743–1794) refuted the phlogiston superstition by the theory that combustion results from the union of oxygen with combustible bodies. Lavoisier, often called " the father of modern chemistry," also revised and improved the nomenclature of chemistry, developed the practice of weighing bodies in explaining chemical reactions, and demonstrated by laboratory method the conservation of matter. In the early nineteenth century John Dalton (1766–1844) developed the atomic theory of matter, formulating the laws of chemical combination. In the latter part of the same century Dmitri Mendeléeff (1834–1907) discovered the periodic law of atomic weights. Recent developments in chemistry have centered around investigations concerning the position of atoms in the molecule, the quantitative treatment of energy relationships, and the internal structure of the atom. Great advances have recently been made in chemistry in the production of synthetic compounds, in the application of chemical knowledge

100

to problems of health and nutrition, and in the improvement of agricultural science.

The values of chemistry, like the values of physics, are far too numerous for citation. First of all, chemistry, like all the studies in the curriculum, brings us knowledge which is vital and interesting for its own sake. Our intellectual curiosity is gratified when we learn what the things about us and in use are made of. It gives us a feeling of confidence to know that we can make and unmake so many of the substances we find in our natural environment. We are thus assured that we live in a world which can be organized to serve the interests and aspirations of man. Our foods, clothes, houses, medicines, tools, and a hundred other articles of daily use possess their present excellence of quality because of chemical research and study. We cannot begin to imagine the convenience and pleasure of living which chemistry will make possible for future human beings. Countless new drugs and perfumes, garments of glass, furniture made of plastics, wool from milk, ready-to-take vitamins, foods in pill form, and higher-test gasolines for our motors — these are but a few of the achievements or promises of modern chemistry. This all brings us back to a warning this book has emphatically submitted: that we must take care that moral insight advances along with technological knowledge. Chemistry, when employed without altruistic perspective, can produce the tools of destruction and death as well as the instruments of happiness and peace.

In addition to opportunities in high-school, college,

and university teaching, chemistry offers vocational careers in research work for governmental bureaus, army and navy, farm organizations, food companies, restaurants and hotels, all types of manufacturing, and various sales positions. Future American civilization is going to be technological in its pattern and motive, and chemists will be necessary to keep its processes provided with the materials of operation.

4. GEOLOGY

Geology is the study of the earth. An enumeration of the various branches of the subject will indicate the objectives of its investigations: (a) *physiography*, the study of the surface features of the earth; (b) *historical geology*, the study of the earth at different historical periods; (c) *mineralogy*, the study of minerals; (d) *petrology*, the study of rocks; (e) *paleontology*, the study of fossils; (f) *economic geology*, the study of the relations of geology to industry, business, and commerce; and (g) *dynamic geology*, the study of the forces which determine the structural features of the earth.

From early times man has recognized fossils as the remains of animals and plants, but only in the modern era has he used them to interpret the evolution of the earth. The traditional tendency to take a literal instead of a spiritual view of the book of Genesis greatly retarded the development and acceptance of scientific geology. James Hutton (1726–1797) was the first to present a naturalistic explanation of geological formations. William Smith (1769–1839) extended further

102

Hutton's thesis that the past history of the earth is to be explained in terms of forces now at work, and discovered, in addition, the fact that fossils indicate the age of rock layers. In the nineteenth century Charles Lyell (1797-1875) became the greatest exponent of Hutton's theory of slow processes in geologic nature, or uniformitarianism. In this century also the findings of geology were linked, in paleontology, to the study of biological evolution. The contemporary outlook of geology is indicated in a mere mention of a few of the fields of its investigations: volcanoes, mountains, earthquakes, plains, glaciers, atmospheric conditions, oceans, plant and animal environments, and mineral and ore deposits.

Geology is an essential subject in the total perspective called liberal education. Without it the student cannot have an appreciative understanding of the earth on which he lives, or of the living forms this earth of ours has produced. Its services to man as an applied science are manifold: the making of maps, the determination of weather conditions, the finding of gas, oil, and mineral deposits, the study of surface formations for agricultural purposes, and the study of atmospheric conditions for aviation and radio — these are but a few instances of geology's contribution to more effective human living.

Geology offers opportunities for a vocational career mainly in teaching, in state and Federal geological surveys, in weather bureaus, in map-making, and in the mining industries.

103

25. *The Sciences*
of the Biological Realm

Biology is the study of living organisms, their nature, structure, continuance, behavior, and evolution. In its biological approach it does not directly attend to the features of living beings which are essentially phenomena for the physical sciences, nor does it deal with the responses of man which are examined in the social sciences. Biology deals with life in its more general and fundamental sense. Especially characteristic of biological science is its elaborate system of classification of plants and animals. The classificatory process includes the following divisions in order of their increasing detail and decreasing scope — phylum, class, order, family, genus, and species. Certain specialized sciences have developed on the basis of their restricted investigation of special phyla. *Bacteriology* and *ornithology* are two well-known examples of these very specialized studies.

The two great divisions of biology are *botany*, the study of plants, and *zoology*, the study of animal life. Botany and zoology may each be studied from several overlapping but quite distinct points of view. These different points of view determine the various subsidiary sciences in the field of biology: (1) *morphology*, (2) *physiology*, (3) *ecology*, (4) *embryology*, (5) *paleontology*, and (6) *genetics*.

1. Morphology, the science of form and structure. Under morphology are *anatomy*, the study of bodies

and their parts in dissection; *histology*, the study of cells as parts of body tissue; and *cytology*, the study of the internal structure of cells.

2. Physiology studies the functions of the different parts of an organism. It is not limited to the study of human beings. Not only does it investigate the larger processes, such as digestion or circulation, but it also examines the minute processes of the cells.

3. Ecology examines the organism in its relations to its physical and biological environments. The influence of environment on habits of living is studied in this branch of biology.

4. Embryology studies the development of an individual organism from the egg to maturity. Embryology embraces the development of both structures and functions of the growing organism.

5. Paleontology studies the remains of ancient animals in sedimentary rocks and investigates the development of species, classes, and phyla. It is interested in the succession and interrelations of different organic types. It was also listed above under geology.

6. Genetics is the study of the hereditary causes of an individual organism's specific character. Its specialty is the study of the transmission and non-transmission of characteristics of parents to offspring. In this science, variation is as important an object of study as heredity.

105

Biology had its roots in Egypt and Babylonia. In ancient times the people of these two countries used plants for medical purposes in a very methodical way. The early Greeks were also versed in the arts of medicine. Aristotle (384–322 B.C.) was the first great biologist. He is famous for the stimulus he gave to scientific observation, induction, and classification, and for his attempt to explain the causes and purposes behind organic evolution. Galen (second century A.D.) was the most important Roman figure in the history of biology. He was the first scientific systematizer of medical knowledge. With the Renaissance came, as great biologists, Andreas Vesalius (1514–1564), the founder of anatomy, and William Harvey (1578–1657), the first to explain the circulation of the blood. Carl Linnaeus (1707–1778), in the eighteenth century, brought into biological classification the use both of genus and of species, and Jean Baptiste de Lamarck (1744–1829) affirmed his celebrated theory of the inheritance of acquired characteristics. About this time also Georges Cuvier (1769–1832) founded the science of comparative anatomy by comparing systematically the structures of living animals with animals now only in fossil remains. In the nineteenth century Charles Darwin (1809–1882) presented his theory of organic evolution by natural selection; Louis Pasteur (1822–1895) promulgated his theories of biogenesis, inoculation, and pasteurization; and Gregor Mendel (1822–1884) brought out his mathematical theory of heredity. Advancement in the life sciences still goes on, with the scholar and researcher

106

delving into the problems of population, nutrition, eugenics, glandular activity, chemical constitution of foods, disease, nervous ailments, sanitation, and many other factors which relate to the life and happiness of mankind.

One of the chief values of biology is its importance for other fields of knowledge. Biology is a basic background for psychology and sociology. Without the principles of physiological behavior discussed in biology these two sciences could derive no sound conclusions. Furthermore, both of these sciences deal with human maladjustments which can be explained fully and finally only in biological terms. Biology, in so far as it relates to problems of race and population, is of direct interest also to history and economics. Literature and fine arts, as concerned with life, cannot ignore the persistent and fundamental principles of the living process. Finally, religion and philosophy, interested in such problems as evolution, freedom, heredity, and communal life, must concern themselves with the pronouncements of the biologist. The practical applications of biology are manifold. The following incomplete list will indicate the importance of biological knowledge in contemporary civilization. Agriculture, forestry, horticulture, animal husbandry, veterinary medicine, medicine, nursing, public health, sanitation, bacteriology, the work of the laboratory technician, home economics, dietetics, research in biological laboratories, and the teaching of biological subjects all represent the importance of this science for intelligent living in modern society. The above

107

enumeration also indicates the opportunities for vocational activity which are available in the biological fields.

26. *The Sciences of the Social Order*

The experiences with which the social sciences deal are as old as man, but the social sciences, as systematic explanations of these experiences, are recent in the history of thought. For several reasons the social sciences have not attained the success and prestige which the natural sciences possess. In the first place, the mathematical physical sciences go back to antiquity for some of their basic concepts and principles. Modern social science was anticipated in ancient thought, but the early social ideas did not possess the validity and objectivity of the early ideas of the physical world. In the second place, the data of investigation in the social sciences are much more complex and elusive. It is very difficult to predict and control in the realm of human behavior. Controlled experiment is seldom possible. In the third place, social science depends largely upon knowledge of the physical world, but a comprehensive and detailed knowledge of physics or chemistry can be obtained without any aid from the social sciences. In the fourth place, the social sciences have to face the problem of human prejudice and self-interest. A man may study astronomy or physics without becoming involved in doctrines which contradict the social opinions of his day, but it is almost impossible for a political scientist or economist to develop his theories without offending some person or organization. The problems of war,

108

taxation, labor, relief, and so on cannot be dealt with scientifically without arousing the opposition of somebody who thinks his rights and prerogatives are being assailed. In the fifth place, social science does not have a great list of inventions and mechanical conveniences to parade before the multitude. Physics and chemistry have made living many times more pleasant and economical by means of technological improvements. The values of the social sciences are not so obvious. They are more intellectual than material. They have to do more with man's habits and purposes, and not with things he owns. In spite of all these handicaps social science has made great strides and is influencing the whole cultural outlook of our day. Social science uses more means of investigation than natural science. Laboratory experiments, statistics, questionnaires, surveys, historical reviews, clinics, psychological analysis, comparative studies — all enter into the social scientist's method of attack. Finally, social science is more concerned than the physical and biological sciences with values and standards. It not only describes the activities of man and his institutions; it also discusses the ideal goals which man should achieve in his social responses. In other words, the social scientist is an interpreter as well as a historian of human life.

The six chief areas of social science are (1) *psychology*, (2) *geography*, (3) *history*, (4) *political science*, (5) *economics*, and (6) *sociology*. Psychology is a science which, because of its great dependence upon physiology, might be classified as a biological or natural as well

109

as a social science. Geography, similarly, has so many relations to geology that it also is sometimes classed with the physical sciences. History is sometimes detached from the social sciences and put in a class by itself. It has a method of investigation which is peculiarly its own, and its purpose is more fundamental and comprehensive than that of the other social sciences. With these introductory comments, let us pass to a brief examination of each of the social sciences which we have selected for discussion.

1. PSYCHOLOGY

Psychology is the scientific study of man's conscious life. This conscious life may be interpreted in purely mental terms or it may be regarded as a name for certain physiological reactions; but in either case it examines human activity and its relation to the environment. Psychology deals with specific and partial responses of the individual; but its main objective is to explain, predict, and control the behavior of the self as an integrated totality. In its investigations and presentations it treats such questions as the following:

What is mind?
What is personality?
How does feeling take place?
How does knowing take place?
What is memory?
What is habit?
Are there instincts?
Do individuals differ in aptitudes and capacities?

110

Psychology follows two methods of investigation: the introspective and the observational. The introspective procedure, usually known as introspection, is carried on when a subject reports his feelings or other mental experiences to the investigating psychologist. This method is inadequate in that it allows prejudice to color the reporting and also in that many subjects cannot clearly describe the contents of their minds, but it does disclose data which cannot be studied in any other way. The observational method, or observation, is used to study the physiological reactions which an individual makes to certain situations. Not only are movements of parts of the body examined as various types of behavior but the structure and function of the parts are also studied. The stimuli which cause the reactions are also carefully described. In carrying out introspection and observation, several procedures are followed: In the *genetic* method the individuals are studied throughout their life history. The *experimental* method applies to psychology the controlled situations and research techniques of the laboratory. Another procedure, *statistics,* involves the gathering and interpretation of data to discover possible correlations between various forms of psychological behavior. Finally, by employing the *comparative* method the psychologist can study the resemblances and differences between two or more behavior situations.

The science of psychology has many subdivisions, the most important of which are as follows: *general, abnormal, applied, animal, child, comparative, physiological,*

111

social, and *clinical.* Various fields are also studied from the psychological point of view in such a way that they come to be regarded as the subject matter of distinct types of psychology. The following are outstanding examples: psychology of aesthetics, psychology of religion, psychology of education, psychology of salesmanship, and psychology of propaganda. Findings of psychology have recently been applied to medicine and to personnel work. Personnel officers in industry, business, education, and social work all apply the techniques of psychology in their counseling and guidance activities. Psychology is related to medicine primarily in psychiatry. In this field, patients are treated for various mental disorders which produce or are caused by physical disorders or social maladjustments. The influence of the patient's feelings, purposes, and memories is closely scrutinized in studying the total background of his unsuccessful response to life situations.

Psychology originated in Western thought in the reflections of Plato and Aristotle concerning the nature of man. These ancient Greek philosophers described the self as a total being with different and distinct functions, and they discussed fully the importance of reason and ideas in the direction of human behavior. At the beginning of the modern era René Descartes (1596–1650) presented the dualistic theory that the bodily processes are purely mechanical, while the mental, as entirely distinct from the physical, nature of man is the purposive and directive agency of the self. John Locke (1632–1704), known as the founder of association psychology, held that all ideas come

112

originally from sense experiences and that complex forms of knowledge are combinations of these basic sensory impressions. A leader in the development of experimental psychology was Ernest H. Weber (1795–1878), who investigated the differences in individuals in the ability to discriminate psychological stimuli. Wilhelm Wundt (1832–1920) advanced psychological science by studying the association function of mind in the formation of words. William James (1842–1910), the psychologist best known to Americans, made great progress in the study of the emotions. He was also famous as a critic of the analytical procedure of the associationists, and developed the pragmatic concept that ideas are functional and operative in the life process. In the analysis of man's inner drives, especially the sex impulse, Sigmund Freud (1856–1939) added a new area to psychological science. William McDougall (1871–1938) gave to the field of psychology a complete classification of the instincts and sentiments of man, and related his classifications to the problems of social psychology. Very recently two new psychologies have been very prominent, *behaviorism* and *Gestalt* psychology. The former, developed especially by John B. Watson, reduces all human responses to physical and mechanical operations — psychology becomes a science like physics, and psychological phenomena are made subject to prediction and control. Gestalt psychology, with Wolfgang Köhler as its chief representative, holds that in perception we do not perceive discrete sensations or isolated data. Separate items are the result of later analysis and

113

discrimination. Perception is fundamentally awareness of patterns or forms of experience known as
configurations.

Psychology has both theoretical and practical values.
Its theoretical importance is found in the contribution
it makes to other fields of knowledge. The significance
of psychology for education is obvious. Without a
definite knowledge of the processes of learning, there
could be no instruction in education or any direction
of the educative process. The economist cannot explain his phenomena without referring to the place
of human interests and wants in the development of
industrial and commercial organizations. Sociology,
as the study of group behavior or the evaluation of
human experience, could not have any foundation
without the presentations of psychology concerning
the origins and standards of knowledge. Philosophy,
furthermore, in its reflections regarding human personality and freedom, would be helpless without the data
of psychology. This discussion of the value of psychology for other fields of study could be carried on indefinitely. Art, literature, morality, religion, dramatics, and marriage — in fact, all the pursuits of man
— depend for their most intelligent employment upon
the principles of psychological science. As an applied
or practical science, psychology is also extensively
beneficial. The control of one's own reactions, the
influencing of another's behavior, the explanation of
the individual and social maladjustments in contemporary society — all require the knowledge and use
of the techniques and formulas of psychology. The

114

spread of propaganda today, the increase in the efficacy of advertising, the growth of commercial amusements, the advancement of psychiatry — all are evidences of the influence of applied psychological knowledge in contemporary living.

Vocationally, psychology offers a background for many different careers. The teaching of psychology, counseling and personnel work, and psychiatry are professions for competent psychologists. Psychological training is also very profitable for the ministry, social administration, journalism, the teaching of philosophy, education, or sociology, diplomatic work, acting, certain government services, medicine, vocational placement bureaus, advertising, writing, and coaching. Research workers in educational and vocational testing and operators in the giving of various tests in schools, correctional institutions, and other places all need specialized training in psychology. Finally, in any vocational field the knowledge of psychology is helpful in the cultivation of successful habits of thought, work, and social behavior.

2. GEOGRAPHY

Geography deals with physical conditions of the earth as they affect the nature and distribution of life. The various activities and associations of man are studied from the standpoint of their relations to environmental factors, like plants, animals, sea, air, climate, topography, and natural resources. The influence of these factors on cultural, industrial, and

115

political institutions is also examined. Geography may follow the general approach of investigating various types of physical conditions anywhere on the earth for purposes of explanation, comparison, and prediction, or the science may restrict itself to the physical phenomena of given regions or localities. For example, a geographer may direct all his research to the investigation of the Rocky Mountains region. Among the several subdivisions of geography the following are the most important: *mathematical* geography, the study of the mathematical relationships between the earth, parts of the earth, and the various heavenly bodies. Under this subdivision the science of *cartography*, or map-making, is sometimes included. *Physiography* studies the influence of the physical conditions of the environment on man and other forms of life. Its researches cover air, water, and land. The influence of the physical environment on plants and the lower animals is treated in *biogeography*. In *human* geography the distribution of man and of the various social organizations is studied in their relationship to environmental causes. *Political* geography examines the locations and forms of government in relation to their geographical situations. Finally, there is *economic* geography, which studies the influence of environmental conditions, such as topography and climate, on man's industrial and commercial activities. Geography is sometimes called a synthetic science, because it employs the findings of many other sciences, including geology and mineralogy, meteorology, botany, anthropology, zoology, and sociology.

116

Like several of the other studies which we have discussed, geography finds its first definite presentations in the theories of the ancient Greeks. Anaximander suggested in the sixth century B.C. that the earth is round, a suggestion fairly well demonstrated by Aristotle (384–322 B.C.). In the development of geographical knowledge the following events were highly significant: the push of Alexander the Great toward India in the fourth century B.C., the trip of Marco Polo to the Orient in the thirteenth century, the discovery of America by Columbus in 1492, the sailing of Vasco da Gama around southern Africa to India in 1498, and Magellan's circumnavigation of the globe in the sixteenth century. In the growth of geography the explorers have had a very important role: Pizarro in South America, La Salle in the United States, Livingstone in Africa, Amundsen in the Arctic region, and many other adventurers in the pursuit of discovering and developing new lands. In the history of geography we find many great geographical scholars. Strabo (63 B.C.–24 A.D.) was the originator of political geography. Philip Cluver, in the seventeenth century, limited geography to a study of the earth and extended the study beyond regions to the whole earth. Bernhard Varenius, in the same century, was the first to systematize geography into its various subdivisions and to relate the subdivisions. Immanuel Kant, in the eighteenth century, further refined the purposes of geography and related it to the study of human experience. Alexander von Humboldt (1769–1859), a great trav-

117

eler, showed the influence of land structures on plant, animal, and human life. Karl Ritter (1779–1859) developed comparative geography by comparing the phenomena of many different places.

Geography is necessary in a liberal education because the history of man cannot be completely understood without definite knowledge of the physical and environmental factors which have conditioned the development of the race and its institutions. Geographical knowledge is also important for the understanding of contemporary human nature. The study of geography broadens one's interests. It informs one regarding the customs, ideals, and religions of other peoples. In a day of international discord and national upheavals geographical knowledge is indispensable for intelligent living. The troubles both within and between the various nations have made us familiar with the whole map of the world. Practically, geography is an essential science for the continuance of modern civilization. The efficient discovery and distribution of natural resources requires the investigations of geography and geology. The location of factories, mines, fortresses, and even cities depends frequently upon the use that is made of available geographical information. There will never be universal peace until statesmen use the knowledge of geography to bring about a just distribution of the mineral and agricultural wealth of the earth.

Two professional fields are open to the trained geographer. First, there is teaching. Geography is taught in almost all schools at almost all levels. In

118

the second place, there are various opportunities in geographical research. Many of these research projects are sponsored by the Federal government, such as those in connection with national parks and reforestation work. Large business corporations, especially those engaged in international commerce, employ the services of research geographers. Geography may be profitable to nongeographers in several ways. The farmer, the journalist, the businessman, the legislator, the diplomat, the novelist, and the engineer will all find geographical information of interest and value in their work. Finally, geography can be of use and fascination to all who travel. The tourist will find that even a very meager understanding of geographical facts and principles will make an auto or railroad trip more meaningful and exciting. The observation of physical phenomena becomes a great deal more significant and enjoyable when we know the laws of these phenomena and appreciate their influence on human life and progress.

3. HISTORY

History is the science which examines in chronological order the succession of human events from earliest recorded times until the present. The main purpose of history is to relate and record events, but it also attempts to explain and connect the happenings in the evolution of humanity. The historian, as historian, is not interested in any metaphysical or supernatural cause of social changes. To the scientific

119

historian, only observable factors in the realms of physical or human activity can be regarded as the determiners of human development. As scientist the historian is not concerned with evaluating the experiences of the race; as a strict historian he is not interested in showing that the historical process has been one of progress, or advancement; with respect to the goodness or badness of humanity's long journey he is neutral. Of course, historians as persons are more than historians, and as persons they have as much right to speculate about the philosophical aims and values of human evolution as anyone else. The student must be careful to discriminate in historical writings between the philosophical interpretations and the scientific observations. As a relater and recorder of human events the historian differs from the chronicler, in that he stresses some events and minimizes others on the basis of their comparative importance. History is frequently used to cover more than human events. For example, we often speak of the history of the world or of the history of life. Finally, it must be recognized that knowledge of man goes back farther than recorded history, as the disclosures of archaeology and paleontology demonstrate.

The main bases of historical presentation are time and place. The chief time divisions are ancient history, from earliest Western records to the fall of the Roman Empire in 476 A.D.; medieval history, from 476 to about 1500; modern history, from about 1500 to the present. The unit of place in historical study is usually the nation, as illustrated by the terms

120

Roman history, *English history*, and *American history*. Often national divisions of history are divided again in terms of time, as, for example, the history of Germany during the Reformation or the history of France during the Revolution.

History differs from the other sciences in that its factual data are not immediately observed. We cannot now hear or see the great episodes of the past. Facts, for history, must be reconstructed from documents, or written statements, which have been handed down as descriptions of past events. The research methods of history therefore center around the criticism of documents. There are two main types of documentary, or historical, criticism: the *lower*, or external, and the *higher*, or internal. Lower criticism seeks to discover the original manuscripts and to translate them into contemporary languages; to corroborate the statements in the original documents by comparing them with assertions in other writings of the same time; and to ascertain the name of the author and the date of authorship of the primary source of information. Higher criticism studies the validity, meaning, and purpose of documents. The higher critic goes beyond the text of the document to discover the social conditions which may have prompted the writing and to ascertain the economic and political consequences of the writer's statements. In higher criticism, investigation also goes beyond the name of the author and the date of authorship to examine the motives and qualifications of the author. Lower criticism represents history mainly as a descriptive

121

science; in higher criticism history assumes the task of evaluation and interpretation.

Among the great historians of all time the following are outstanding: Herodotus (*c.* 484–425 B.C.), known as "the father of history," wrote comprehensively and artistically regarding the ancient world. Thucydides (*c.* 460–396 B.C.), another ancient Greek historian of superior literary excellence, and the earliest exponent of the scientific method in history, introduced the notion that history should bring moral teaching into the recording of events. Tacitus (55–120 A.D.) was a Roman historian, noted for the brilliance and objectivity of his writings. Augustine, bishop of Hippo (354–430), one of the earlier theological historians, interpreted the historical process as the unfolding of the will of God. Forerunners of scientific history in France and Italy, respectively, were André Duchesne (1584–1640) and Muratori (1672–1750). The eighteenth century produced some of the greatest of the modern historians, namely, David Hume (1711–1776), Edward Gibbon (1737–1794), G.W.F. Hegel (1770–1831), Turgot (1727–1781), and Helvetius (1715–1771). Hegel regarded history as a process of opposing movements, or dialectic, whereby the Absolute and Universal Idea is realized in social institutions, especially in the state. Turgot explained history in terms of moral and psychological laws, while Helvetius believed that social institutions and sociological conditions are of main importance. The nineteenth century saw the rise of these historical scholars: Thomas Carlyle (1795–1881), Henry Buckle (1821–

122

1862), Karl Marx (1818–1883), and Leopold von Ranke (1795–1886). Carlyle held that great men are the chief factor in the determination of historical events. Buckle believed that the chief determining factors in history are food, soil, and the other physical conditions in the geographical environment. Marx adopted Hegel's theory of the dialectical method in history, to explain the development of historical processes and institutions on the basis of economic want in human nature.

The discoveries and interpretations of history become the subject matter of many other sciences regarding man. There could not be social science without history. Anthropology, sociology, political science, and economics base a large part of their findings and conclusions on data assembled by historians. Literature, religion, and philosophy would be meager pursuits, indeed, without the content furnished in historical writings. History is culturally important because it enables us to understand the institutions of our modern life. It traces their origin and development in such a way that we can fully appreciate their merits, defects, and objectives. History also introduces us to the great heroes of the race and shows the importance of leaders in human progress. An interpretative study of history can help contemporary man in selecting the forces and conditions which shall determine future social development. The thoughtful and objective study of history can also warn us against the political, economic, and other environmental forces which in the past have brought despair and destruction to the race. An appreciation of history increases our interest in current events, the material of tomorrow's history. Approached with historical perspective and appreciation, the daily newspaper, the book of the month, the latest play, and even the textbooks of a college course take on meaning and vitality. And here a note of caution is necessary: We must not carry the lessons of history too far; we must not make the events of the past reflect values and goals which they never possessed. History must not be used for false and dangerous propaganda. When nations, in the guise of patriotism, twist the events of history for a greedy and violent purpose, history degenerates from a science into black art and magic.

History, as a profession, is open to comparatively few persons. The teaching of history in high school, college, and university is the main vocational opportunity in this field. Historical scholars are sometimes employed to prepare historical articles concerning the growth and activities of institutions. Governments and religious organizations are the main institutions employing historians for this purpose. Historical knowledge is a very great asset in many professions. Librarians, dramatists, novelists, essayists, and statesmen all use to advantage the presentations of this science. Finally, history is of value and pleasure to every citizen. The dynamic and human way in which history is now presented in biographies, movies, plays, novels, and even in scholarly treatises makes preoccupation with this subject one of the most lively and profitable activities of hurried modern living.

124

4. POLITICAL SCIENCE

Political science studies the nature and function of civil government. It examines social organization and the problems of order and disorder within any societal group. It is concerned with the institutions and practices which produce or express political power. Its chief concern is with the great and dominant powers in society, namely, national governments; but it studies minor powers as well, as, for instance, the township or county. In its scope it even extends beyond national powers to discuss the interrelationships between nations and the possibilities of international political organization. In its purely scientific perspective it examines political institutions from a neutral and objective point of view. Monarchies and dictatorships are just as legitimate a part of its subject matter as democratic governments.

Political science is distinguished from sociology in that it studies only those social activities which have to do with government. It is closely related to economics, the science which studies the problems of wealth, in that political and economic issues frequently overlap. The economic tendencies and consequences of the New Deal indicate very clearly why political science may have to use some of the principles of economics. Like all other social sciences, political science depends largely upon the data of history. Without historical knowledge a study of the evolution of government and a comparative examination of various political orders would be impossible.

125

Political science employs several methods of investigation. We have just referred to the *historical* approach. The *descriptive* method describes in detail the different political institutions and activities. Another method, the *statistical* method, seeks to find mathematical correlations between the many complex factors in government and between governmental activities and other social processes. In some cases the statistical method in political science is concerned merely with the enumeration and tabulation of governmental activities. Political science is again sometimes studied from the standpoint of *law*. Frequently, political processes cannot be studied without a clear understanding of the principles which underlie them. It is very difficult, for example, to understand American political institutions without a legal study of the Constitution. The method of *interview* and *questionnaire* is another technique in political science. In this approach the political views of individuals of various walks of life are investigated. Finally, there is a *philosophical* point of view in political science. This standpoint is followed when the political scientist wishes to evaluate the processes of government from the standpoint of a world view or a moral theory. It is fair to say, however, that political science is primarily concerned with the processes of government as they actually exist and not with how they ought to exist. In other words, political science is usually a descriptive science. It is the function of social ethics, rather than that of political science, to attempt the moral or philosophical evaluations of governmental institutions.

126

The main divisions of a curriculum in political science are these: *comparative government*, a study of various past and present political orders; *municipal government*, the study of city politics and administration; *political theory*, the study of the principles, functions, and objectives of governmental processes; *public law*, the study of the legal instruments and procedures which prevail in governmental administration; *international relations*, the study of the political activities which occur in and because of the interactions between nations; *public administration*, the study of the organizations and techniques in the operation of governmental agencies. Any inclusive curriculum in political science would, of course, study also such topics as political parties, public opinion, state government, the courts, elections, and legislative procedures.

The history of political institutions contains the record of many great social changes. Back in antiquity there were the reforms of Solon (*c*. 639–559 B.C.), who started the first democracy in the Western world. Then there was the founding of the Roman Empire in 27 B.C., which arose as a revolt against despotic senators, but which, in its own time, degenerated into outright tyranny. Following the fall of the Roman Empire in 476 A.D. the so-called Dark Ages, the medieval period, emerged, with its church control, political organizations, and feudal economic institutions. The crowning of Charlemagne as Holy Roman Emperor by Pope Leo III in 800 A.D. was the pre-eminent expression of centralized authority and papal power in the Middle Ages. With the signing of the Magna

127

Charta in 1215 English monarchy received its first constitutional limitation. Also in the thirteenth century not only Parliament, but also the democratic aspect of Parliament, the House of Commons, came into being. In the seventeenth century, with the crowning of Louis XVI and James I of England, the rise of strong nation-states began. In the eighteenth century the paramount event was the complete separation of the United States from England with the establishment in America of a democratic republic. The nineteenth century brought great reforms in democratic voting in England, the abolition of slavery in both England and the United States, and the founding of the German Empire. The present century has already witnessed the rise of communism in Russia, the first World War, the establishment and disintegration of the League of Nations, the emergence of Fascism and Nazism, the establishment of autonomous dominions in the British Empire, the invasion of China by Japan, and the second World War. The years immediately before us are bound to bring political activities of momentous importance to the future of the human race.

Among the great political theorists in the history of Western civilization the following have been most famous and influential: Plato (427–347 B.C.), who argued for a just and aristocratic state in which reason would be supreme; Aristotle (384–322 B.C.), who followed, in the main, the political ideas of Plato, but who advanced political science through a widespread investigation of the political constitutions of his time;

128

St. Augustine (354–430 A.D.), who held that the principles of the City of God should apply in earthly political organizations as they prevail in heaven. Thomas Aquinas (1225–1274) emphasized the necessity of holy insight in the minds of rulers and the importance of reason in the creation of laws. Hugo Grotius (1583–1645) was an early advocate of international law, arguing that justice between nations is based on the nature of things. Thomas Hobbes (1588–1679) held that people were under contract to obey their rulers, arguing that only in such obedience could they escape the dangers and fears of the brutal state of nature. John Locke (1632–1704), a proponent of natural rights, affirmed that no one ought to injure another in the enjoyment of life, health, liberty, and property. Locke, like Hobbes, held to a contract theory of government; that is, he believed that people, for their own protection, should agree to establish and obey laws. Locke did not agree with Hobbes, however, that the monarch had unlimited authority. A contract theory which allowed still more privileges and rights to the people was that of Jean-Jacques Rousseau (1712–1778). Karl Marx (1818–1883) held that the development of political institutions is a continual struggle between economic groups or classes, and in his theory the working class, because of its size and natural right to the products of its labor, will ultimately come to political control. The philosophy of Marx was a theoretical basis of the communist state founded by Lenin in 1917. The ideologies of Mussolini and Hitler, threatening as they are to democratic institutions, cannot be omitted from the role of political theories which have influenced the historical process. We have indicated their effect on the culture of democracy in another section of this book. Finally, we have the name of Franklin D. Roosevelt, President of the United States, a social idealist who has tried to preserve the fundamental values and principles of a free capitalist society, while at the same time he has encouraged the adoption of radical and sweeping social reforms.

Political science offers its main professional opportunity, of course, to teachers in this field. In the high school, college, and university, courses are offered in the various divisions of this science. Training in political science has, however, many other vocational uses. Newspaper reporting, editorial writing, the work of the radio news commentator, religious missionary work, consular service, and commercial law all require a considerable understanding of political processes. The chief users of applied political science are the men and women who occupy executive, legislative, and judicial positions in our government. From a ward committeeman up to the President of the United States an intelligent appreciation of political principles and procedures is an indispensable prerequisite in the preparation of public servants.

The values of political science in a liberal outlook are manifold. A man cannot be a good citizen without an understanding of the political activities of his local community, state, and nation. Every businessman must know the legal requirements and implications of his vocational pursuit if he is to be successful in his enterprise. The American citizen's knowledge of political science today must extend far beyond a knowledge of the political processes of his own nation. He must understand the political ideologies and procedures of all the great nations of the world if he is to take an intelligent part in promoting the welfare of his own country and the peace of all peoples.

5. ECONOMICS

Economics is a science which studies the ways in which man produces and uses wealth. It examines the methods by which he obtains a living in business and industry. In its investigations it also concerns itself with the social conditions which both promote and follow the production of wealth. Economics has both theoretical and applied aspects. As a theory, economics seeks to discover the laws and tendencies which underlie economic phenomena. As an applied science, economics employs its facts and principles for the organization and control of economic processes. Money, banking, public finance, and transportation are examples of the applied functions of economics.

As has already been indicated, economics is closely related to political science. Trade, currency, prices, wages, and so on are affected greatly by governmental systems and regulations. Economics, again, has a close connection with sociology. It may even be considered as a branch of sociology which considers certain phases

131

of man's total social activity. Without history economics would be deprived of a large part of its subject matter. The study of economic history and economic institutions would be meager pursuits without the material made available by historians. Geography also has an important bearing on economics. The production, transportation, and distribution of material goods is conditioned to a great extent by such factors as soil, climate, contour of land, and other factors of the physical environment. Economics also influences the social philosopher in his reflections concerning the ideal social order. Finally, economics employs psychology in that many economic attitudes and practices are determined by the psychological wants and habits of man.

The following list of questions indicates the kinds of problems with which the economist is concerned: What is wealth, and how is it produced? What is interest, and how is a just rate of interest determined? What is rent, and how is a just rate of rent ascertained? What are the rules governing the value and use of currency? What determines the price of goods? How can the social problems which result from unemployment, unjust distribution of goods, large national debt, and labor troubles be solved? How can farmers secure a reasonable return for their labor without dangerously raising the cost of living in the cities? And, finally, what are the psychological and moral factors which most greatly affect economic competition?

A brief summary of the main concepts in the development of economic science will be of interest:

132

In the sixteenth century Sir Thomas Gresham (1519–1579) discovered the law that bad money tends to drive good money out of circulation. By bad money he meant money which has relatively little intrinsic value, as, for example, paper money which cannot be redeemed for its value in gold or silver. Gold is a good example of good money, because it has value in itself in addition to its worth as money. Turgot (1727–1781) discovered the law of diminishing returns, which holds that eventually, through intensity of exploitation, the results achieved are not commensurate with the effort. The physiocrats, of whom François Quesnay (1694–1774) was a leader, defended the theory that land is the only producer of wealth. Adam Smith (1723–1790), often considered the founder of economics, discovered the important role which labor plays in the production of wealth, but he gave due credit to the productive values of capital and land. An outstanding theory which fitted in very well with the theory of natural selection in evolution was that of Thomas Malthus (1766–1834). Malthus argued that population tends to increase according to a geometric ratio, whereas the means of subsistence increases merely according to an arithmetical ratio. This idea has been discredited as a completely true interpretation, but it is a basic point of view in the study of population problems. David Ricardo (1772–1823) propounded the famous " iron law of wages," which affirms that the absolute minimum rate of wages is that which enables workers to live, marry, and bring up children. Ricardo is important also because of his theory that rent is not determined so much by the profit made from land as by the scarcity of land. In the nineteenth century an outstanding discovery in economics was the theory of "marginal utility," which asserts that the price of an economic good is determined by the minimum degree of utility which will cause continuance of its production or use. Alfred Marshall (1842–1924) was the first to point out in economic theory that the moral qualities of individuals have productive economic value. John Stuart Mill (1806–1873) also brought ethics and psychology into the economic picture by evaluating men's pursuits in terms of their power to promote the happiness of the people. Finally, Thorstein Veblen (1857–1929), leader of the institutional school of economic theory, presented the important conception that individuals are more effectively motivated by habit and custom than by reason.

The science of economics has important consequences for contemporary civilization. Pressing problems like unemployment, low agricultural prices, and business depressions cannot be solved without a thorough and sound knowledge of economic principles. Other serious social situations, like population pressure, delinquency, crime, and poverty, are largely economic in their nature and must be met by social scientists and statesmen well informed in economics. The continuance of beneficial social institutions, like the state, the school, and the church, is dependent upon economic conditions. The world situation today, with its wars and rumors of wars, is a glaring testimony

134

to the importance of economic considerations in international relations. When it comes to the industrial and commercial pursuits that make up the vocational life of most of our citizens, the importance of economic principles is obvious. Finally, all of us, as consumers, are greatly concerned with the problems of price, income, and taxation. It is small wonder that some social philosophers have interpreted the entire evolution of human society on the basis of man's economic urge and behavior.

The science of economics is probably more significant vocationally than any other social science. In addition to the teaching of the science in high schools, colleges, and universities, economics offers professional opportunities in the following pursuits: in agriculture, in the activities of rural economists, county agents, and other social technicians dealing with farm life; in statistics, for research workers with governmental agencies, business corporations, and research foundations; and in the field of accounting, for certified public accountants in governmental business and legal areas of work. Economics is also a very valuable intellectual asset for editorial writing, research work in all of the social sciences, social service, and the practice of law. In fact, every citizen, whether he is a businessman, farmer, student, or statesman, needs for effective individual and social living a working knowledge of economic facts and principles.

6. SOCIOLOGY

Sociology is frequently known as the science of society. It is the study of the origin, laws, and functions of the various human groups. As a theoretical science it seeks to discover the laws that underlie human organizations and their interrelations. Its theories are largely based upon principles arrived at in history, political science, economics, and the other social sciences. As an applied science it applies the facts and laws of social phenomena to control the activities of man in his different groupings. For example, criminology is sociology in one of its applied aspects.

Other sciences are often listed as divisions of sociology, although they have distinct contents and principles of their own. Among the social sciences frequently included in sociological study are the following: *anthropology*, the study of man and his origins; *ethnology*, the comparative study of various cultural institutions during the evolution of society; *anthropometry*, the science which measures the physical characteristics of representatives of the different cultures; and *social administration*, the technological application of sociological knowledge, by institutional organizations, to the handling of the social problems of contemporary society. Closely related to sociology in its studies are comparative religion, social philosophy, and social psychology. Sociology divides its investigations into specific areas of study, as the race, the family, the school, and the church. Poverty, crime, class conflict, and other social problems which

136

relate to human beings as parts of societal groups receive the scientific examination and the remedial services of sociologists. Case studies, life histories, historical comparisons, statistics, and experimentation all enter into the sociologist's investigation of social phenomena.

Until the rise of modern scientific thought sociological knowledge was mainly expressed in the writings of philosophers, religionists, and historians. In the eighteenth century social reflections took on a more definite specialized and scientific character. The Encyclopedists of France were leaders of the movement to explain and control social processes by the methods of reason. Voltaire (1694–1778) and Saint-Simon (1760–1825) were outstanding thinkers who tried to separate social theory from religious interpretation in order that human institutions might be given an objective and rational explanation. Auguste Comte (1798–1857), known as "the father of sociology," was the chief social philosopher to investigate social processes in a strictly scientific way. He claimed that social science, like physical science, should be factual and observational, or, as he put it, positive. He insisted that social theory should abandon its theological and metaphysical presuppositions and assume the methodology and spirit of natural science. In the nineteenth century four social thinkers presented conceptions which reflected a definite scientific purpose and pattern, namely, Herbert Spencer (1820–1903), Émile Durkheim (1858–1917), Karl Marx (1818–1883), and Gabriel Tarde (1843–1904). Spencer described society as an organism, and explained the development of social institutions according to the same principle of increasing heterogeneity which he ascribed to inorganic and organic processes. In the light of this principle he believed that humanity was passing from a homogeneous society to a pluralistic democracy. He also held that social evolution followed laws of natural necessity and that progress is inevitable. Needless to say, recent developments in our international social order have demonstrated the inadequacy of Spencer's theory. Durkheim, accepting in principle the organic theory of society, believed that society determines the actions of its members in the same way that an organism conditions the behavior of its parts. The influence of the total society on the individual is expressed in customs, rules, and laws. Marx emphasized the influence of groups on each other, and pointed out how each social group, or class, sets up an ideology, or a system of beliefs, to justify its own aims and activities. Tarde answered the theories which emphasized the determining force of the total society by affirming the power of the individual to influence the ideas and processes of the group. The scientist who is called " the father of American sociology," Lester F. Ward (1841–1913), accepted, for the most part, the standpoint of Tarde. Among recent sociologists the names of W. G. Sumner, W. I. Thomas, F. H. Giddings, and A. W. Small have been outstanding.

Sociology is practically and vocationally valuable in all pursuits which deal with social relations, and this means almost all the interests of man. The journalist, statesman, novelist, historian, economist, clergyman, and personnel officer especially need to know the observations and conclusions of sociology. Sociology as a specific profession is open to teachers of the subject, workers in the field of social service and institutional administration, and research experts in bureaus which study the social processes and problems of a city, state, or nation. To the general student or average reader sociological writings bring interesting and valuable information. They tend to give him an unprejudiced and comprehensive view of the institutions of which he is a part. They help him to escape pernicious propaganda, and may prevent him from supporting causes and organizations which are detrimental to human welfare. As a citizen he is given important knowledge for voting and other civic responsibilities. In sociological discussions he learns what the serious social evils of the day are, and of ways to remove them from his environment. The enlightenment he receives regarding the plight of the underprivileged and the handicapped members of the race deepens and broadens his sympathies and develops his capacities for tolerance and understanding.

27. *The Humanities*

I am using the term *humanities* in a very loose way. Originally the humanities were studies of the masterpieces of classical culture. The literatures of Greece and Rome in the beginning constituted the humanities. In the Middle Ages the designation *humanities* was applied to secular culture as opposed to divine, or theological, knowledge. With the rise of the modern educational era the humanities came to include all the studies which embrace an understanding of civilization. Recently, however, since very definite classifications have been made, to include, respectively, the natural sciences and social sciences, the division of humanities has taken over cultural studies not contained in the other groupings. With this rough and practical usage of the term in mind, we shall discuss in the present section (1) *literature*, (2) *fine arts*, (3) *music*, and (4) *philosophy*. These studies, more than any others in the curriculum, deal with man's inner intellectual enjoyment and purpose. They present to the student the ideals and standards of good taste. The humanities are his introduction to the world of aesthetic appreciation, cultural insight, and moral aspiration. They will not show him directly or definitely how to make a livelihood, but they will instruct him in the noblest of all arts, the making of a life.

1. LITERATURE

Literature is the written expression of the best ideas of mankind. In carvings, inscriptions, manuscripts, and books the literary heritage of the ages is preserved. By literature is meant the writings that have permanent value and appeal for readers of all times. Through literature the culture of the race continues and progresses. Each generation cherishes and preserves

140

the literature of the past, and at the same time adds to man's total culture by creating literary masterpieces of its own, though there have been periods of creative sterility in the literary history of all peoples. Literature is the manifestation in writing of man's imaginings, emotions, and reflections about life. Literature is more than the reflection of the mind of the author; it discloses the spirit and life of the author's epoch, nation, and civilization. Poems, songs, dramas, and stories are more than the reflection of an individual mind, even though that mind be that of a genius; they are the revelation of the fundamental soul of the race.

The study of literature is not identical with the study of language. All literature is language, but not all language is literature. For example, scientific treatises, government reports, and textbooks are presentations in language, but rarely are they literary works. Good literature always requires the correct use of language. A definite working knowledge of *syntax* and *grammar* is essential. *Rhetoric*, or training in the art of expressive speech, is also indispensable. Competency in literary *composition* is a still further advantage in developing sensitivity to fine literature. The ability to read foreign languages understandingly broadens the field of one's literary knowledge and appreciation. Acquaintance with *philology*, the study of the development of language, makes possible a more intelligent understanding of the meaning of literary presentations. The study of *comparative* literature also increases the reader's capacity to understand and enjoy. Finally, a working knowledge of the

141

methods of literary *criticism* enables one to evaluate the purpose and worth of an author's work. Intelligent enjoyment of literature, in short, requires much more than the ability to read with accuracy and speed; it calls for an appreciative understanding of all of the arts and principles of human language. If students recognized the importance of this fact, there would be less protest against courses in composition, logic, and foreign languages.

Literature is not restricted in its subject matter as are the specialized intellectual pursuits. It is free to enter the field of science, philosophy, religion, history, sociology, fine arts, or any other area of human interest. Furthermore, there is a freedom in the method of literary expression which is not enjoyed by other departments of learning. The methods of scientific investigation or of philosophical speculation are limited and prescribed. The literary author, however, is at liberty to follow his creative imagination to its fullest expression. The writer is also free to present his own hopes, prejudices, and feelings with an abandon unknown to the natural or social scientist. This is not to say that literature is without any restrictions or principles. Imagination may be free, but it should not be absurd or offensive. However creative the author's work may be, it can never be good literature if it violates the basic principles of aesthetic taste or moral decency.

A hasty review of some of the world's literary masterpieces will suggest the significance of literature in our cultural heritage. Western literature began

142

with ancient Greece. Homer's Iliad and Odyssey, the tragedies of Aeschylus, Sophocles, and Euripides, and the dialogues of Plato all reflect the literary genius of the Greeks. After the decline of Greece, Roman literature arose with the works of Vergil, Horace, Ovid, Terence, and Cicero. To the Middle Ages belong the romances of King Arthur, the stories about Charlemagne, the lives of the saints, the *Canterbury Tales* of Chaucer, and, as the literary climax of this period, the *Divine Comedy* and other poems of Dante. Then the Renaissance brought into the literary tradition of the race the marvelous creations of William Shakespeare. The seventeenth, eighteenth, and nineteenth centuries, manifesting in turn the moods of reason and romanticism, nourished the literary genius of Milton, Voltaire, Rousseau, Pascal, Pope, Goethe, Shelley, Keats, Wordsworth, Byron, Scott, and Tennyson. The last decades of the nineteenth century, reflecting the growth of industrialism and scientific knowledge, have brought forth Nietzsche, Zola, Ibsen, Maeterlinck, Hauptmann, Anatole France, and H. G. Wells. Our survey must not limit itself, however, to European authors. American literary history also contains many illustrious names. Jonathan Edwards, Thomas Paine, William Cullen Bryant, Ralph Waldo Emerson, Nathaniel Hawthorne, Henry Wadsworth Longfellow, Edgar Allan Poe, James Russell Lowell, Walt Whitman, and Mark Twain are but a few of the poets, essayists, and novelists who have given our nation a literary influence and tradition. As the college student surveys

143

the development of literature in the various countries he will realize that one book has appeared in them all and has kept its prestige and influence throughout the centuries — the Holy Bible.

The cultural values of literature are too broad and diversified for brief reporting. First of all, literature helps us to appreciate the inner nature of ourselves and others. It helps us to understand and control our profoundest desires, prejudices, and hopes. Aware of the conflicts and struggles in our own deeper experiences, we tend to become sympathetic and tolerant. Literature helps, therefore, to join people of various races and creeds in a single fellowship, based on the recognition of our common human nature. In the second place, literature liberates the spirit of man. It frees us from humdrum existence, it gives wings to our imagination, it discloses the dignity and significance of life, and, in its most tragic portrayals, even reveals the beauty and sublimity of natural and human events. Finally, literature is instructive and informative. Appealing to the emotions as well as to the intellect, it gives us knowledge of man and nature that is stimulating and vital. Biography, history, and even philosophy, when written with literary enthusiasm and style, make learning a delight.

From the standpoint of vocational success, education in literature opens the way to several important professional fields. The teaching of English in the elementary grades, high school, or college; newspaper work; continuity writing in radio; authorship of poems, essays, stories, dramas, or books; making advertising copy; library work — all require persons with literary background and training. The ministry, public speaking, salesmanship, and law also require workers with a sound working knowledge of the English language. The ability to read and speak foreign languages is advantageous in many professions. Foreign correspondents, diplomats, interpreters, executives in international business, directors of travel agencies, army and navy officers, radio commentators, and translators of foreign documents and books all require for professional success a working knowledge of at least one language other than English. Only a person who knows the language of many peoples can ever be truly a citizen of the world.

2. THE FINE ARTS

In the history of culture the fine arts have included architecture, sculpture, painting, music, and poetry. Usually, in the curriculum of a liberal college, the term *fine arts* does not include architecture, music, and poetry. It is used, rather, in the conventional way in which the term *art* is employed. In this book I am referring to the fine arts in the latter, or limited, sense. By fine arts I mean sculpture and painting, and associated pursuits like drawing, ceramics, costume design, and stagecraft.

The term *fine arts* always refers to the creative works of man that record his aesthetic emotions. The creations in the field of the fine arts, such as a beautiful painting or statue, appeal to our sense of beauty.

145

Not all beautiful objects, however, are works of art. For example, the view of a distant mountain may be an excellent example of beauty, but it would be artistic only if its beauty were reproduced in picture form. Art always refers to the creations of man and not to those of nature, however aesthetically pleasing natural phenomena may be. Unlike the useful, or mechanical, arts, the fine arts are not judged on the basis of their power to advance the material interests of man. An artistic object possesses an intrinsic value of its own, namely, its beauty; the money it may bring to the artist does not affect its real, or artistic, value. It is to be recognized, however, that many objects may be both useful and beautiful at the same time; often the fine and mechanical arts blend in an artistic creation, as in the making of a beautiful rug or a graceful vase.

Although the fine arts are associated primarily with objects which have a value and importance in and for themselves alone, the fine arts, as activities of man, bring him many benefits which go beyond the field of art. In the first place, the arts are physiologically beneficial. They afford him a way to release pleasurably and profitably his excess energy; they are an admirable type of recreation. In the second place, a thing of beauty may be also useful for daily life. Weapons, houses, boats, and other instruments of community life may draw upon the fine arts for their form. In the third place, the fine arts have an educative function. In pictures and sculpture the various groups of mankind have passed on from generation

146

to generation the traditions and purposes of their people. In the fourth place, in creative and artistic activity a man or woman realizes the value and dignity of his individual personality. In producing a valuable work which will survive long after his death, the artist realizes the power, glory, and permanence of human selfhood. Finally, art has a great socializing influence. It appeals to the universal and basic emotions of all mankind. The beauties of great painting and sculpture, like those of great music or literature, not only dispel conflicts and jealousies but afford a common ground of enjoyment and fellowship.

The history of sculpture and painting is replete with the creative achievements of man. A brief list of his creations will indicate the glory and originality of his artistic genius. In sculpture an ancient Greek, Phidias, gave to the race the frieze of the Parthenon; Praxiteles, also of Greek antiquity, carved out the matchless statues of Hermes and Aphrodite; in the Renaissance, Michelangelo produced the wonderful statues of David and Moses. With the coming of modern times Jean Houdon arose as the great portrait sculptor of France; Christian Rauch appeared in Germany as the founder of the Berlin School; in England the period of naturalistic sculpture emerged with Alfred Stevens and Thornycroft; and in America, Saint Gaudens and Lorado Taft, both modernistic in style, were among the most important. Among recent artists in this field the most influential has been Rodin, of France, who was supreme in the expression of psychological feelings in sculpture.

147

Painting did not originate as a separate art. In early Greece it was used in the beginning as an aid to sculpture and architecture. Painting was done in ancient Rome in the decoration of houses and tombs. During the Middle Ages the religious motive prevailed, and the paintings were colorful and decorative. The sixteenth century saw the rise of several great Italian masters of painting, among whom were Raphael, Leonardo da Vinci, Michelangelo, Titian, and Tintoretto. In the seventeenth century, in the northern part of Europe, were the famous artists Rubens, Van Dyck, Frans Hals, and Rembrandt; in the same century Spanish painting flourished in the works of Velásquez and Murillo. Among the celebrated painters of the last three hundred years have been Watteau, David, Millet, and Corot, of France, and Hogarth, Reynolds, Turner, and Constable, of England. Van Gogh, of Holland, Picasso, of Spain, and Bellows, Curry Benton, and Wood, of the United States, have been leaders in the twentieth-century movements in painting.

From the standpoint of their cultural significance the value of the fine arts is obvious. Like literature and music, the arts of sculpture and painting broaden the scope and depth of our experience. They add to the enjoyment and interest of life. Like religion, they disclose the possibilities of the human spirit; they reveal the capacities of man for appreciation, sympathy, and originality. With an understanding of the fine arts the citizen of today can feel at home in the galleries, museums, universities, and other cultural centers where the works of great artists are displayed. The fine arts also offer many opportunities for enjoyable and profitable vocational life. Teachers are needed in this field, as in all other curricular areas of high school and college. Expert knowledge of design is valuable in textiles, plastics, ceramics, jewelry, interior decoration, and costuming. Commercial drawing provides opportunities in cartooning, magazine illustration, advertising, and the movies. Occasionally the position of director of an art gallery is available to a person competent in the fine arts. In the libraries of our large cities and universities members of the staff are frequently chosen because of their specialized knowledge of painting, sculpture, and the other arts. Finally, the fine arts are not without financial reward from the standpoint of individual creation. Only a few artists can expect great monetary compensation for their work, but there are enough commercial opportunities in these pursuits to encourage the proficient sculptor or painter to make art his only profession.

3. MUSIC

This is not the place to present a technical examination of music. It is sufficient to say that music is the art of combining tones, either by voice or instrument, to produce a melody and harmony for the emotional enjoyment of the hearer. Music has several unique characteristics. In the first place, it is temporary. Except as it is recorded in written symbols, or notes,

149

music is fleeting; its sounds soon pass away. Quite different is the permanence of a statue or painting. In the second place, music rarely copies or reflects nature. Musical compositions seldom remind one of the objects or happenings of life about us. They represent the freest use of man's creative imagination. In the third place, music is only slightly intellectual. Its aim is to arouse feelings, not ideas. Unless joined with words, as in an opera or anthem, it does not reproduce any knowledge which may be in the mind of its composer. The composer's joy, sorrow, pity, or fear may be reflected in his music, but the music by itself will not tell why the composer is thus emotionally aroused. In the fourth place, the products of musical composition are not immediately available to the beholder. We can enjoy directly and at once the poem of an author or the picture of a painter, but the written music must be translated into vocal or instrumental sound before we can enjoy it. The fact that a piece of music may be sung or played by different people permits the same music to be performed in many places — an advantage which can never be enjoyed by a work of painting or sculpture.

In the music curriculum of a college or university several different topics are taught. The student is given ear training; he is given an explanation of scales and chords; he is informed regarding harmony, as the relationship between simultaneous tones, and counterpoint, the art of plural melody; the physiology of the vocal organs is thoroughly presented; the various musical instruments are described; and the ways to

150

appreciate and evaluate good music are indicated. The student is also shown the relationship of music to other studies. Since the medium of music is sound, the student of this art will be instructed in physics, especially in acoustics. He will learn about drama and poetry, because they join with music in opera and song. He will also learn about the human body, because it is so closely associated with music in the art of dancing. Moreover, he gains a deeper understanding of religion through the study of church music. Again, in philosophy the student of music will attend to aesthetics, the science which studies the fundamental principles and problems of all the arts. Finally, by surveying the history of his subject the student will become acquainted with the contribution of the great composers to the development of human culture. When he studies the music of Germany the names of Bach, Handel, Haydn, Mozart, Beethoven, Schubert, Schumann, Mendelssohn, Liszt, Brahms, and Wagner will mean something definite and significant. In the roll of Italy's masters of music he will appreciate the genius of Scarlatti, Palestrina, Rossini, Bellini, Verdi, and Puccini. He will become acquainted with the works of Chopin, of Poland, and Tchaikovsky, Moussorgsky, and Rimski-Korsakov, of Russia. Finally, the name of MacDowell, the famous American composer, will remind him of America's prominent place in the ever-enlarging tradition of music.

Education in the theory and practice of music is of powerful cultural significance. In the music of a

151

people we experience the fundamental desires of their hearts. Like literature, and much more forcefully, music is the reflection of the spirit and idealism of an epoch. In music man finds release from the restrictions of drab, everyday, routine living. In song he finds courage, peace, and hope. This does not mean escape, a flight from reality; it means that with music in his heart man can tackle the exacting problems of modern life with confidence and faith. Like the other arts, music not only brings men and women individual enjoyment and strength; it also brings people together in a common fellowship, based on a universal interest of the human spirit. Vocationally, the opportunities of music are many. There is, first, the teaching of music, vocal and instrumental, in schools or at home. Again, there is vocal or instrumental work in churches, on the radio, in theaters, and in orchestras. There is also a field for vocal and instrumental concert soloists, directors of choirs and orchestras, and singers in opera roles. Again, the newspapers and magazines offer opportunities for musical criticism. Finally, the composing of music, both classical and popular, is a vocation of importance in American professional life.

4. PHILOSOPHY

The purpose of this section is to present a statement of the meaning and function of philosophy in contemporary civilization. I shall refrain from recommending any one philosopher or any one philosophical

152

system. I shall suggest, rather, the great objectives of thought with which all interpreters of life and reality, whether idealists or materialists, humanists or supernaturalists, must be concerned. I am giving additional attention to the place of philosophy in the curriculum because the essential aims of philosophical study are the ends which should characterize all departments of learning. The liberal tradition throughout the history of thought has been stimulated and sustained by developing arts and sciences which have been true to the philosophical ideals of unity, inclusiveness, and validity. In emphasizing the philosophical perspective in higher learning I do not claim that this standpoint is found only in the philosophy curricula. Teachers of science, art, literature, religion, and all other studies, when they follow the cultural ideal, manifest a zeal for the philosophical standards of knowledge.

At the outset I should like to remove certain frequent misconceptions of philosophy.

In the first place, philosophy is not, by any means, idle speculation removed from all connection with the actual experiences of man in the realms of science and social living. The notion that a philosopher lives in a make-believe world of fanciful abstractions is pure superstition. All the great philosophers started out on their intellectual quest after intimate and rigorous association with the world of actual facts. Plato was a mathematician, Kant an astronomer, Leibnitz a botanist, Spinoza a physicist, Locke a medical scientist, and James a psychologist. Anyone who thinks of

153

philosophers as idle dreamers and otherworldly dispensers of intellectual " moonshine " should remember what Cicero said about Socrates. " Socrates," asserted Cicero, " called down philosophy from heaven, settled it in cities, and introduced it into home life, making it the pretext for many questions on life and morals." There have been philosophies of the mystical and intuitive sort which have advertised immediate access to divinity by supernatural methods; but in the main the road of philosophy has been, to use the language of John Fiske, " through nature to God."

In the second place, philosophy is not the attitude of resigning oneself to circumstances and indulging in dramatic heroics in the face of difficulty and danger. Some of the noblest of the philosophers have used their philosophy as an instrument of courage in the time of distress and defeat, but it has often been the case that philosophy has led serious-minded people to rebel against the injustice of nature and to propose drastic programs for the reconstruction of the world. Some people, as Robert Louis Stevenson pointed out, take philosophy like a pill, and those who do, he added, manifest a forlorn stupidity. Shakespeare notwithstanding, philosophy has a nobler purpose than simply to be served as the " sweet milk of adversity."

In the third place, philosophy is not the same as religion. It is true that in American colleges and universities the professors of philosophy have frequently been clergymen and that many of the great problems of philosophy are identical with those of religious theory; but increasingly the teachers and scholars in

154

philosophy are entering this enterprise from the backgrounds of literature or the sciences. Many laymen have paid a great deal of attention to the religious aspects of philosophy because they have become alarmed at the detrimental influence which philosophy sometimes has upon immature thinkers. " A little philosophy inclineth a man's mind to atheism," Francis Bacon did assert, but he also declared that depth in philosophy brings it back to religion again.

In the fourth place, philosophy is not, as a great many suppose, a futile controversy about questions which men can never solve. Being based upon individual reflection, philosophical knowledge is of course controversial. There are so many different perspectives from which the great issues of philosophy may be approached that variation in theories is inevitable. But philosophy has made progress, not only toward unity and harmony in its doctrines, but also in the clarity and validity of its main affirmations. Philosophers still argue over such problems as the nature of the soul, the reality of God, and the meaning of happiness, but the definitions and solutions of these problems presented by thinkers today have an instructive and convincing character not even hoped for in the reflections of the past. Speaking technically, the doctrines of neutral monism, emergent evolution, and logical positivism are philosophical achievements which are purely modern in motive and expression.

The protest of Omar Khayyám still continues as an unconscious prejudice against philosophy in the minds of many.

155

Myself when young did eagerly frequent
Doctor and Saint, and heard great argument
About it and about; but evermore
Came out by the same door wherein I went.

I might cite other criticisms and taunts directed against philosophy. Cicero said, "There can be nothing so absurd but may be found in the books of the philosophers." Goethe, in his *Faust*, calls the philosopher " a beast on a blasted heath, led round in a circle by an evil spirit." Keats declares that philosophy will clip even an angel's wings. But in the last analysis, to philosophers themselves we must go for the worth and joy of the speculative life; and they will agree with Plato — in spirit, if not in letter — that philosophy is the music of the gods.

Philosophy, as a profession, is open only to teachers of the subject in colleges and universities, or to philosophical writers in the field of literature; but the layman, who does not desire to be a professional philosopher, somehow or other feels that the philosophical mood is greatly to be desired in the thought life of the day. The ordinary man's attempt to find out what goal of living is the best for human behavior, his search for unity and design in the hodgepodge of contemporary knowledge, his aspiration to find in these days of economic and political uncertainties the ultimate purpose and goal of civilization, his search for an intelligent and harmonious basis for religion in a day of vague and contradictory theologies, his longing for a rational sanction for personal and social morality — these and many other serious enigmas

156

cause him to develop, more surely and effectively than he himself realizes, the philosophical temper. We are beginning to realize, as men have always realized in times of transition, confusion, and distress, that the philosophical vision, usually thought so impractical and otherworldly, is man's wisest and noblest guide to a revitalized and reconstructed civilization. As Professor Montague has recently asserted, philosophy may be poor in proof, but it is rich in vision; and vision is what we desperately need today.

The question immediately arises, What kind of thinking must be developed if the philosophical response to life is to be inculcated in our citizens. I suggest five marks of the philosophical mind; or, to use the etymological meaning of the term *philosophy*, I wish to submit five characteristics of *the love of wisdom*. Philosophical knowledge is *fundamental, universal, systematic, critical*, and *personal*.

By saying that philosophy is *fundamental* knowledge, I mean that it is concerned with two ancient questions, both of which have to do with the ultimate nature of the world. The first query is that of *first cause*. What is the world? What is it made of? Whence does it come? What is the primordial stuff? Is the substance of the world matter, mind, spirit, God, or what? It is this question, technically one of the problems of *ontology*, or theory of being, which historically brought philosophy close to theology and which now is carrying it right into the arena of the physical sciences, with their investigations into the

157

ultimate constitution of reality. The second question of philosophy as fundamental knowledge is that of *final cause*. Here we have the problems of *cosmology*. What is the drift of things? Is the world moving toward some far-off event? Is there a persistent and dominant purpose in the universe? This question also has made philosophy seriously interested in the biological sciences, with their theories about the nature and destiny of evolution. At first blush it seems that these questions of first cause and final cause are purely academic and abstract speculations; but a great many philosophers believe — and with good reason, I think — that the everyday attitudes of an individual toward his family, his community, his vocation, and other concerns of his life depend a great deal upon the reactions which he experiences as he thinks or refuses to think these questions through.

The second main characteristic of philosophical knowledge is its *universality*. It wants to know not only whence the universe came and whither it is going but also what kind of universe it is during the process. Is it material or spiritual in its chief essence? Is it one or many? Is it good or evil? Is it evolving or static? Philosophy is also universal in that it includes anything and everything in its deliberations. As somebody has said, philosophy is the Sears Roebuck of the intellectual world. The real and the unreal, the true and the false, the significant and the insignificant, the visible and the invisible, all have a place in the speculations of the philosopher. Again, philosophy is universal in that, like pure science, it seeks the

158

widest and most inclusive principles for the interpretation of particular events.

The third feature of philosophical knowledge is its *zeal for system*. To use an expression of Bertrand Russell, the philosopher is driven on by " the system-maker's vanity." Philosophy is the integrator of all other fields of knowledge, the co-ordinator of all theories. It seeks the principles of nature which are beneath and beyond the laws of the specific sciences and tries to suggest the great purpose which includes in its comprehensive design the particular objectives of the minor and separate events of the world. A. N. Whitehead, the great Harvard scholar, formerly of Cambridge University, suggests that the study of philosophy is a voyage toward the larger generalities — a voyage in which we endeavor to frame a coherent, logical, necessary system of general ideas in terms of which every element of our experience can be interpreted. In short, as Herbert Spencer has affirmed, philosophy is completely unified knowledge.

The fourth mark of the philosophical mind, the *critical attitude*, stresses the fact that the thinker must base all his reflections upon accurate definitions and valid assumptions. This was the great role of Socrates in the Athenian state. He insisted that men should think with clarity, consistency, and sincerity. The interest of the philosopher in sound methods of thought represents his concern for the rules and practices of *logic*. Out of this interest has grown the philosopher's work in *epistemology*, that is, his quest for the meanings, origins, and standards of effective human knowledge.

159

This interest of philosophy in logic and epistemology has made it very valuable as an instrument to prevent both extreme dogmatism and extreme skepticism in man's intellectual behavior. Philosophy stands, on the one hand, for positive convictions and assurances, and, on the other hand, it supports the place of doubt and questioning in our mental processes; but it insists that both convictions and doubt shall flourish in a spirit of tolerance, patience, and rationality.

Nowhere is the critical attitude of philosophy more needed than in the political life of our citizenry. Our democratic tradition and idealism will have neither the purpose nor the power to endure unless the American people prove themselves intellectually and morally worthy of participating in the administration of the inevitably complicated technological society of the near future. As Professor Charles A. Ellwood has pointed out, " Democracy in a complex society such as ours depends absolutely upon the culture and enlightenment of the masses." There must be a democracy of brains, as well as a democracy of ballots, if democratic institutions are to survive.

Two serious defects in the attitude of the American people today keep them from the philosophical type of intelligence and character necessary for effective popular government. In the first place, the average American is too prejudiced and compartmental in his thinking. Our stubborn allegiance to the doctrines of competitive business, sectarian religion, departmentalized education, and partisan government is symptomatic of the partisan nature of our national

160

mind. We have many scholars who can describe and criticize the distinctive activities of industry, education, or politics, but we drastically need thinkers who have the ability to construct out of the conclusions of specialized social inquiry a synoptic view of social life as a whole. However valuable the methods of specialization may be in the sciences of physical and mechanical phenomena, in the interpretation of the living " social tissue " they are false and dangerous. In deploring the conflict of social opinions I do not mean to decry all differences of intellectual outlook. Any social theory which attains oneness through flagrant and arbitrary disregard of real opposition is morally as well as logically indefensible. But if social theory is to evoke a unified social life, the different points of view must be integrated and reconciled, as far as possible, so as to form one harmonious and inclusive vision. There will always be many different tactics and maneuvers in the drive for social and moral truth; but, to use the words of Professor Durant Drake, there must be " a general map and chart of action."

The second weakness of the general reflective response of the American people is its impetuous and opportunistic character. Urged on by the exigencies of trying times, we glorify the novel, the speedy, and the practical in economic, political, and educational procedures. Disillusioned by the pathetic breakdown of old theories and customs, we have developed a cynical and supercilious attitude toward the entire meaning of the past. This widespread mood of

161

skepticism toward tradition has purged our national spirit of the sham and sentimental values of historical perspective in social interpretation. There is, of course, good reason for the lack of comprehensiveness and profundity in our social thinking. Times of emergency naturally provoke radical and untried measures. In the main this impulsiveness of spirit is wholesome and constructive. But we need to remember that a radical social vision which, in its enthusiasm for material profitableness and speedy workability, ignores the continuous underlying principles of the total mind of the race is an empty and deceptive dream.

From a consideration of philosophy as critical reflection, we pass to the fifth characteristic of philosophy, namely, its *personal perspective*. This is indicated in several ways.

To begin with, the philosopher wants to know what personality is. What is soul? What is mind? What is consciousness? This is the age-old question of speculative psychology. This is the old body-mind problem of traditional psychology.

Secondly, he is interested in values — truth, goodness, beauty, and friendship. And no sooner does he get into a discussion of these great values than he finds that they are always the objective of some personal desire or appreciation. No philosophical quest is more insistent or fascinating today than this search for the meaning, ground, and authority of values — logical, aesthetic, ethical, cultural, social, religious, and so on. Technically this pursuit of philosophy is called *axiology*, which means theory of values.

162

A third way in which philosophy raises the question of personality is in its reflections about God. Is the universe personal? Is there a rational, benevolent mind at the center of things? This also is a very pressing question in contemporary reflection and appears in religious discussion in the debate between the humanists and the theists. Problems like these are the burden of the *metaphysics of religion* and *theology.*

Fourthly, the personal character of philosophy is disclosed in the problem of man's relation to his cosmos. Will brute force or personal values ultimately triumph in the system of things? This question is, as you know, the problem of pessimism and optimism, and it is the question which most people regard, and rightly so, as the most important and rewarding inquiry of all reflective excursions of man. A sound optimism about life is like fire insurance. If there is no disaster, it may never pay dividends. But if tragic circumstances arise, it is a heartening and profitable compensation. The problem of pessimism and optimism in philosophy, when translated into the ideas of religious thought, becomes the perennial question of the necessity of evil.

Finally, philosophy as personal is concerned with the relations of human selves to each other in community life. The economic, political, and social institutions of the day all represent reflections or conditions of an individual philosophical outlook. To present a rational and compelling philosophy of civilization is one of philosophy's supreme tasks in this era of rival doctrines of civilization and government. *Ethics* and *social philosophy* are the studies which concern themselves with these questions of human organization and conduct.

In the history of philosophy the names of certain great thinkers stand out. Without attempting to list all the most influential philosophical scholars of Western culture, I submit the following as highly significant and influential: Plato (427–347 B.C.), whose doctrine of perfect and eternal ideas largely became the basis of Stoicism, Christian theology, and modern idealism; Aristotle (384–322 B.C.), who brought the principle of purpose into the evolutionary process and made the ideal of self-realization the principle of moral and social progress; Aquinas (1225–1274), the supreme expositor and systematizer of scholastic Catholic philosophy; Descartes (1596–1650), the founder of the skeptical method of inquiry and the first modern to propound the dualism of mind and body; Thomas Hobbes (1588–1679), the materialist who reduced everything to physical motions; Baruch Spinoza (1632–1677), the first great scholar to employ the principles of mathematics and mechanism in the formulation of a naturalistic pantheism; John Locke (1632–1704), the great empiricist, who found the beginning and basis of all human knowledge in sense impressions; George Berkeley (1684–1753), the pre-eminent idealist, who reduced all processes, physical and physiological, to mental contents; Immanuel Kant (1724–1804), who found the laws of scientific phenomena in the innate forms of human understanding, and who proclaimed the free, moral will

164

as the foundation of ethics; Georg W. F. Hegel (1770–1831), the absolutist in philosophy, who interpreted reality as an all-inclusive, rational whole, whose universal perfection is the result of a progressive dialectic within the finite parts; John Stuart Mill (1806–1873), the utilitarian, the exponent of happiness as the criterion of moral and social goodness; Herbert Spencer (1820–1903), who employed the conclusions of all the sciences of his day to construct a complete evolutionary philosophy of life and the world; and, finally, William James (1842–1910), the American psychologist and philosopher, who formulated, in the doctrine of pragmatism, a working conception of truth. Among contemporary philosophers John Dewey and William E. Hocking are distinguished leaders.

No thinker has quickened and cleansed the imagination of man more gloriously than the ancient martyr sage of Athens named Socrates. I close my discussion of the college curriculum with an admonition from this noble thinker, whom Xenophon called the happiest and best of mankind; and what Socrates says regarding philosophy is true of every course of study in a student's college program. These are his words — words which will remain an eternal challenge to all seekers of the truth: " Do not mind, Crito, whether teachers of philosophy are good or bad, but think only of Philosophy herself. Try and examine her well and truly, and if she be evil try to turn all men from her. But if she be what I believe that she is, then follow her, you and your house, and contentment will delight your heart."

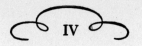

IV
THE ART
OF SELF-DENIAL

OBLIGATIONS
OF LIBERAL EDUCATION

A GREAT religious leader, the apostle Paul, once affirmed that, even if a man had all knowledge, his knowledge would be nothing without love. Ideas of scholarship, divorced from ideals of sacrifice, may become instruments of oppression and autocracy. The purpose of the rest of this book is to show that unselfishness is an essential attitude in the liberal view of life. Without altruism there could be no democracy, and without democracy the liberal perspective would vanish from the thought and language of man. This need for sacrificial motives in democratic behavior brings us directly to the moral issues in educational theory. Only individuals with ethical insight can possess the sympathy and imagination to relate their own private interests to the welfare and happiness of all. What, then, are the moral principles which underlie an altruistic philosophy of life?

28. *The Postulates of Intelligent Morality*

Socrates was one of the greatest ethical and educational leaders of antiquity, if not of all history. His views of personality, morality, government, philosophy, science, and religion will influence human thought for all time. For our present consideration I select two ideals of Socrates which are fundamental and

169

essential in any moral theory of education. These two ideals, or postulates, of Socrates are: (1) *There can be no wisdom without virtue*, and (2) *There can be no happiness without wisdom*. Both these assumptions are contrary to the cynical views of the worldly-wise skeptic. To the blasé skeptic only the stupid are virtuous, and only fools are happy. I wish, however, to suggest some ways in which these Socratic tenets are both true and useful.

1. The principle that there can be no wisdom without virtue, or, to put it in other words, that a man has to be good in order to be wise, is valid and valuable on two counts.

a. In the first place, our moral outlook determines the types of intellectual objects we select for our attention. The college youth on a visit to a large city does not prefer a burlesque show to a Shakespearean drama because he is ignorant. No, he attends the burlesque because, for the occasion, he allows a lower moral interest to alter his normal perspective. Colleges will never turn out lovers of the true, good, and beautiful in literature, art, music, and science until higher education concerns itself with the development of high moral taste in the preferences of youth. It is the pure in heart who see God. Yes, and it is also true that only the pure in heart see anything with honesty and clarity. The scientist who lies and cheats in his personal and social relations will some day discover that he has lost his power to discriminate between the true and the false in the laboratory. The

170

jealous and hateful individual soon loses his capacity to discern the potential goodness of the human soul. I am not saying that a college student with a lewd and selfish outlook cannot pass his courses. I must admit that he may actually graduate with high honors. I do assert, however, that his total perspective will have been too clouded and contaminated with improper ideas to permit the more sensitive and noble appreciations which grace the superior understanding.

b. In the second place, the principle that virtue is a prerequisite for wisdom is highly important in selecting the permanent objectives of one's educational career. The selfish and materialistic student will choose one program of studies; the altruistic and idealistic student will select another type of curriculum. Interest in studies and, consequently, appreciation of their content vary directly with the significance one thinks the studies have for later professional life. Courses in biology and chemistry, which would be very interesting to a student of medicine, would have much less attraction for a student of music or foreign languages. In the light of Socrates' dictum, the best way for a student to enjoy all the courses in his curriculum is to background them with the moral purpose to live a life which will command the broadest intellectual outlook. Or, to put the principle another way, whenever a student attains the ethical desire to achieve the most complete, unified, and proficient type of personality possible, all the studies in his schedule take on meaning, usefulness, and appeal.

171

2. There are also two reasons for believing in the Socratic principle that there can be no happiness without wisdom. One of these reasons lies in the fact that there cannot be *liberty*, one great highway to happiness, without wisdom. The other reason lies in the fact that *loyalty*, the second great highway to happiness, also depends upon wisdom for its success.

a. The happiness which comes with liberty may be of three kinds. It may be the joy which comes with *creativity*, as in writing a book, painting a picture, composing a song, or inventing a machine. Again, the happy experience may come with *contemplation*, as in the ecstasy which accompanies the listening to a beautiful symphony, the observation of a golden sunset, or the meditation of a prayer. Finally, there is the pleasure which comes with *control*, as in the scientific manipulation of the physical environment, the organization of a social movement, or the disciplining of one's own desires. Common to all of these three means to happiness is the requirement of knowledge. One cannot create intellectually, contemplate aesthetically, or control technologically without a fund of lively ideas. If liberty is an essential of happiness, Socrates was certainly correct in declaring that there could be no happiness without wisdom.

b. Loyalty, as the second essential of happiness, is based on the moral and religious principle that the man who lives for himself alone can never enjoy the abundant life. It is expressed in the paradoxical thesis that whoever loses his life shall find it. The realization

172

of this principle in practice requires the attainment and employment of extensive knowledge. People cannot be loyal without two types of information. First, they must understand fully the situations which demand their service and sacrifice. The loyal person must sympathetically know the depth and scope of human need and suffering. One of the great omissions of liberal education in the past has been its indifference to problems of social wrong and injustice. The college of today must come down into the market place, open its eyes to dirt and squalor, and cry out for reconstruction and reform. Only when college curricula contain courses about human evil and pain will college graduates be motivated to discover the happiness which comes with serving the common good.

The second type of information which the loyal man must possess is that which will show him the way to make his loyalty effective. Preaching, advice, and sympathy can never solve by themselves the baffling problems of social wrong. Sacrificial motive must be joined with scientific method. Medicine, sociology, statistics, government, education, economic planning, and all the other instruments of social control must be made available to the modern saviour of mankind. Again Socrates is right: there can be no happiness without wisdom.

I need not tell my readers that the postulates of Socrates regarding wisdom, virtue, and happiness are not widely influential in American ethical theory and practice. They are recognized — when recognized

173

at all — as interesting speculative ideals, with little relevancy to the actual conditions of human living. When one seeks the cause of our inadequate moral philosophy, one explanation stands out. It is the unwarranted assumption, frequently present in contemporary ethical theory, that when people become intelligent regarding the causes and effects of human behavior, they will necessarily follow the dictates of their intelligence. As a result of this belief we have falsely taken the spread of knowledge and education to be a sign of universal goodness. We have become too optimistic about the moral stamina and idealism of America. We need to realize that our great technological advancement has not automatically brought ethical strength and excellency. Let us examine this deceptive belief more fully.

29. *A Common Mistake in Ethical Thinking*

The error referred to above can also be stated as the notion that no person knowingly does wrong. It is as old as the doctrine of the ancient Greek Sophists, who declared that virtue can be taught like any other subject. The victims of this old fallacy seem never to realize that morality is not fundamentally something a man learns. Morality refers to what a man is — his aims, his character, his being. This cannot be learned like arithmetic or geography; it is a quality of selfhood which develops through inner purpose and not through external stimulation. Morality has more to do with what a man does with education than with

174

what education does to him. As has already been emphasized, there cannot be wisdom without virtue.

Although I admit that the ignorant or foolish man cannot be effectively good, I do not believe that intelligence is the complete or final remedy for moral inadequacy. In the first place, a large part of our population has not been educated to a degree of profundity which would give it the right to free ethical expression. Furthermore, on the basis of this belief there could be only a relative and pluralistic moral system. When biologists and psychologists convincingly affirm that intellectual abilities are different in all individuals, we cannot have the universal intelligence which would be necessary for a common moral code. If the way to morality is the way of knowledge, then the intellectuals must become the arbiters of ethical theory and practice. This is the road to dictatorship by a privileged class. An aristocracy of brains is better than an autocracy of bullets, to be sure, but a democratic people can never be ruled by a few, however wise and benevolent the few may be. The way out of the pluralism and relativism of a democratic ethics is not through the leadership of an élite minority but through allegiance to the mores and ideals of the many. The prophet and the statesman can always bring new conceptions into the social mind, but these innovations can never exert authority in a democracy until they win the approval of the majority of the people. This means that a democracy must move slowly and inefficiently; but it also means, and gloriously so, that in a democracy the individual still

175

has a voice that is influential and free. Only in such a society can liberal education have any reason, purpose, or power.

Another objection to the belief that no man knowingly does wrong is the fact that people who know all the drastic consequences of a condemned course of action do not refrain from pursuing it. Inform the youthful follower of crime about the dangers of wickedness, describe the horrible prospect of years in prison, emphasize the false glamour of the gangster, yes, tell him again and again that crime does not pay — and the young man may still risk the ways of lawlessness. The carnage and unrest which prevail throughout the world today are indisputable evidence that modern scientific knowledge is not a guarantee of human justice and happiness. I acknowledge that prudence and foresight are necessary and useful in the moral life, and I admit that the ethical adventurer is more apt to be a reckless fool than an audacious saint; but I insist that the function of intelligence in morality is regulative, rather than stimulative. Intelligent fear of syphilis may keep a man from becoming a degenerate roué, but it will not give him the positive idealism which causes a faithful husband and father to sacrifice his very life for his family. Do those who practice predatory business methods know that co-operative economic planning would be much better both for industry and for the public than a system of cut-throat competition? Of course they do. Their hesitancy to welcome new socialized forms of business administration is not due

176

to ignorance; it is due rather to selfishness and greed. Human society is not reverting to barbarism today because of any lack of knowledge, science, or technology. The great failure of modern man has been his inability to direct his technical skill with humanitarian moral purpose. As the contemporary philosopher Bertrand Russell has pointed out, knowledge must be blended with love if society is to be saved.

This is all by way of saying that, however proficient the machinery of social control may be, the redemption of civilization will never be effected until there is inculcated in the private individuals who administer the technological instruments of social salvation the spirit of courageous and disinterested service. The best technical and scholarly information in the world may be available for us; but if we have not the spirit of altruism, it will profit us nothing. It is not the place of morality to furnish mankind with intelligences able to grapple with the perplexing problems of our modern industrial society; but it is emphatically the responsibility of the ethical interests in life to give to the intelligences capable of solving the difficulties of today a passionate concern for the public good.

The real guides of moral living are not academic students of ethics, whose knowledge of ethical theory is based almost wholly upon library or clinical research, but the heroic souls who, in the midst of danger, disease, and death, patiently and painfully toil for a better world. Learned and technical treatises on ethics do have, of course, a great influence on the formation of acceptable moral ideals, but scholarly

177

dissertations on morality can never drive man to a burning stake or a crucifixion hill.

What has this plea for moral aspiration to do with the processes of liberal education? A correct and expected answer is, Continue instruction in the history, theory, and application of ethics. Another reply, and one more desperately needed, is, Give greater recognition to teachers who in their private and professional lives exemplify the ideals of honesty, purity, and unselfishness. The teacher speaks much more loudly in what he is than in what he says. I earnestly believe that instructors in our colleges and universities should be more honored for their moral effect on the lives of students than for laboratory research or literary productiveness. If a college professor wishes to judge the efficacy of his own work, let him note carefully the number of alumni who visit him from time to time, who write him for advice, or who recall with gratitude an inspiring word spoken in a class hour years ago. When all is said and done, it is the unconscious influence of the professor upon his students which gives to liberal education its most potent force in the life of the community. I am supported in this conviction by the words from the book of Daniel which are inscribed on the obelisk at the grave of the philosopher Fichte: " The teachers shall shine as the brightness of the firmament, and they that turn many to righteousness, as the stars that shine forever."

30. *Liberal Education*
and the Tasks at Hand

This book has portrayed fully the broad, sweeping vision of liberal education. It has been very free in its presentation of general principles and universal ideals. I wish at this point to indicate the function of liberal education in the situations of immediate, everyday life.

What educators need today in our educational objectives is a sincere zeal to disclose to students the actual world in which they live. There is a time for speculation, but there is also a time for rigorous, critical analysis. Perhaps we shall serve humanity best if we clearly disclose, without fear or prejudice, the relativistic mind of our restless and confused era. If we honestly portray the economic and political disorders of our day, the thinkers of tomorrow, recognizing our plight, may be provoked to resolve the contemporary hodgepodge into some form of cultural and communal order. In any event, the interpreters who shall come after us will be spared the ignoble enterprise of erecting a philosophy of life upon the shaky foundations of wishful imagination. The age of Plato and Aristotle was culturally superior to the period of the Sophists, all will admit; but the glorious epoch of the Academy and the Lyceum would have been impossible without the provocative preparatory era of Sophistic criticism.

Wrapped in extravagant reflections about society at large, or reality as a whole, and attaching our idealism

179

to causes far beyond our reach, most scholars fail to attain the feeling of adequate individuality which comes with the actual accomplishment of a specific moral objective. I do not mean to detract from the high importance of philosophical and scientific seers who have the intelligence to comprehend wide fields of experience, but they ought to recognize that the majority of students will have neither the opportunity nor the capacity to control the destiny of man by sweeping generalizations about society or nature. There is, of course, a need for the training of leaders with a world vision, but we must remember also that the masses of men have a right to guidance in the local issues of their daily living.

In fact, it may well be argued that the best way to develop thinkers of far-reaching insight is to cultivate the power of thought in the problems of everyday life. It is culturally profitable for students to be interested in the questions of cosmic evil or international unrighteousness, but for the sake of their present personal satisfaction and future social usefulness the ethical thinking of students must be directed to the understandable and manageable problems of lawlessness in their own campus groups. Teachers would also enjoy the exhilaration of social service much more intensely if they would more frequently supplement their theoretical endorsement of some world-wide cause with earnest, sympathetic attention to an immediate ethical need in their own home town. The academic scholar has traditionally been too prone to treat apathetically the humdrum problems of his next-

180

door neighbor. The quickest and surest way for a student or professor to justify his education in the opinion of the townspeople is for him to sympathize with them in their troubles and to co-operate with them in their local programs of community building. There is no finer or better way for a scholar to exemplify the spirit and purpose of liberal education than by being a kind and helpful friend to the people of his own home town. Educators need to be reminded not only that culture, like charity, must cover the world but also that culture, like charity, should begin at home.

This discussion of the educated man's duty to his fellow man raises the question as to the marks of a good personality in democratic society. What kind of person is most admirable and most valuable in a democracy? Or, to put the question in educational terminology, what ideals of thought and action should the liberal college seek to develop in the individual student? In reply to this query I suggest four objectives for a liberally educated person. They are more than aspirations; they are duties which any enlightened citizen will recognize as his legitimate obligations to the social community. These ideals or responsibilities of a proficient personality are *physical well-being, social responsiveness, religious idealism,* and *comprehensive understanding*. Let us examine them in turn.

181

31. *The Right to Be Strong*

Interest in the physical well-being of the American people means a great deal more than curing the sick, feeding the hungry, and clothing the naked. It means fighting with all our powers the evils of poverty, slum life, child labor, disease, narcotics, intemperance, war, and scores of other social perils. It means championing legal and educational policies which will make it unlawful for those who are physically or ethically incapable of normal parenthood to enter upon this sacred and momentous endeavor. It calls for the promotion of the type of family and neighborhood life in which boys and girls will have a fair chance for bodily care and development. Concern for the health of American citizens will require levying increased taxes upon those with great wealth, in order that public parks, playgrounds, clinics, dispensaries, and hospitals may be provided for the masses who live in penury. It will mean the abolition of all businesses in which unscrupulous men make fortunes by selling to the multitudes harmful foods or drugs. Zeal for the health of the citizenry is a moral necessity if the people of America are to have the strength and stamina to defend themselves in time of war. Might doesn't make right right, but it does make right strong. In short, the promotion of the public health is no ordinary and trivial cause. It is an enterprise which can demand to the limit the altruism, ingenuity, and courage of a crusading spirit.

Soup, soap, and salvation — these are sometimes called the threefold offerings of the Salvation Army. The order of their benevolent services is unassailable. To save a man when he is hungry and dirty is not even good taste. We have to rid ourselves of the historic prejudice about physical well-being and bodily vigor. We are still under the influence of the puritan, ascetic conviction that bodily health and beauty are grossly inferior to other human values. We need to realize openly and gladly that physical culture is a value in and for itself. We need to appreciate the worth of mere living.

We no longer treat our bodies as the slaves of our immortal souls, but we treat them as slaves in a less admirable sense. We have made health the tool of social attractiveness, sexual power, and professional ambition. We take tons of powder and pills, we gargle rivers of mouth wash, we use up mountains of soap. The reason is not an appreciative interest in the intrinsic artistic merits of the human body. More customers, higher wages, better social connections, more flattering compliments — all these are the things which make the American people by the millions groom their bodies with the ardor of zealots. We need to teach folks to play for the sheer love of the game, to show them how to be healthy for the very joy of living, to inspire them to behold the human form without lustful imaginings. Goals like these, and not vulgar display or selfish advantage, are the ideals of true social vision in the realm of physical living.

183

With more and more leisure becoming possible in this technological age, public education in the best use and enjoyment of physical recreation is one of the most imperative obligations of our social order. We need to realize, with Stuart Chase, that " what the age of machinery has given us in time, it will fain take away again by degrading the opportunities which time affords." The machine has brought us leisure, but it has also brought us commercialized athletics, jazz dancing, speedy automobiles, sexy movies, blatant radio programs, and other obstacles to cultural and self-initiated recreational behavior. Machine-made amusements have a rightful place in American life, of course; but when they stifle the ardor of the people for personally created or improvised play activities, the moral stamina of the nation is in danger. The chief menace to the play life of a people is the tendency to be a mere onlooker, or spectator, rather than a participant in the arena of recreation.

No period of human history has ever surpassed in the brilliance of its culture the Golden Age of Greece. But, then, no people has ever learned to play with the originality and abandon of the ancient Greeks. The Greeks, with their concern for total personality, taught the world that intellectual achievement and social responsibility are futile without the physical grace and strength which come with the participation in competitive games. We might even add that no nation can truly pray if it does not really play.

184

32. *Essentials of Social Competency*

Social responsiveness, the second mark of effective personality, has three major phases: *enjoyment of normal family life, economic self-respect and security,* and *political participation and responsibility.*

As indispensable for the development of individual personality through good home life, I mention four needs in the contemporary status of the American family. First, a sane, constructive, courageous attempt to limit by the best instruments of biology and sociology the birth of hopelessly unfit offspring. Second, a thoroughgoing analysis of the growing divorce evil from the standpoint both of spiritual objective and of scientific explanation. Third, an extended movement to educate youth in the values of personal and social morality. Fourth, a conscientious attempt to conserve in our modern industrialized, mechanized urban civilization the ancient art of gracious fellowship between parents and children. The home must remain the basis and center of social happiness and good will.

The second phase of the adequate social experience of an efficient citizen is economic security. This ideal calls for a good deal more than the extension of public charity. The American who would economically help his financially underprivileged fellows must do much more than give a donation to the community chest. He must fearlessly examine our entire economic system with its attendant social evils. If he is sincere in his profession of moral idealism, he will scrutinize the concentration of America's wealth and power in

185

the hands of a few people; the unemployment of millions of men and women; the inhuman housing conditions in our larger cities; the strife between capital and labor; the use of children in industry; the wastes of war; and many other economic dangers no less destructive to society.

By political responsibility, the third phase of social responsiveness, I mean the right and duty of individuals to have a voice in the determination of public policies. I venture to protest against the extreme collectivistic and autocratic drift of contemporary political theory. I admit that the present-day American democracy is notoriously sluggish, careless, wasteful, and corrupt. I also acknowledge gladly that the tendencies toward socialization in our government mark, in the main, progress toward justice and happiness. I am convinced that to governmental control of industry and commerce and to state ownership of many forms of production we shall have to look if we are to eradicate the ills of our present society. What concerns me is not the objective of contemporary collectivism but the methods whereby this objective is to be attained. The socialized state should appear through the willing co-operation of its constituents. This means that the process will be one of slow evolution and persistent and patient education. In times of peril and distress there may be valid grounds for autocratic measures; but there is always the danger that autocratic policies, recognized as valuable in times of stress and strain, will become the regular procedures of normal times. To sacrifice liberty for

186

prosperity has always been the cardinal temptation of political and economic man. We need desperately to realize that without democracy civilization cannot survive. For democratic government is the only form of political rule in which the civil liberties, like trial by jury, freedom of speech, the right of assembly, and freedom of religion are safeguarded.

Whatever the future governmental system of America may be, we shall never have social order and proficiency until the citizens who make up the state have the sacrificial spirit of good will and altruism. There can be no effective community life if the spirit of community is not in the minds and in the hearts of the masses who make up the community. And how can we cultivate this spirit of community? By presenting to the ordinary citizen obligations which he can actually carry out. As I have already asserted, the way to develop a sense of social responsibility is to show the average man the need of public service in his own vicinity. The way to save the world politically, as well as religiously, is to start at Jerusalem, then go to Samaria, and only later move on to the uttermost parts of the earth. I do not wish to detract from the value and glory of prophets of international social vision, but for most of us our chief ethical service to humanity will have to be rendered in our own local community. To help clean up the vice in one's own ward is just as noble as to talk learnedly about purity in some far-off land. We cannot develop a real and intelligent sense of responsibility toward the nation and the world until we are aroused to care

187

about the shortcomings in our own home towns. Local government by work is better than international government by talk.

33. *Religious Idealism in the Liberal Outlook*

The third great privilege and duty of the liberal self lies in the area of religion. The social force which gives motivation to all other interests of man is religious aspiration. And when I speak of religion, I mean no dogmatic, sectarian view. I refer to the general response which may be known as faith in the highest human values. What this type of confidence implies can be shown by indicating the major affirmations of the religious tradition.

In the first place, religion emphasizes the importance of personal moral character without which all ethical enterprise must lack honesty and persistence. There is no more powerful impetus to altruistic endeavor than the high esteem for the personality of others which comes with consciousness of one's own moral integrity. Good politics without good people is an impossibility. America needs to be saved from poverty, disease, vice, crime, and a host of other evils; but the only permanent way to eradicate them is to remove greed, dishonesty, lewdness, and other human sins from the minds and hearts of individual members of the race. The quest for personal holiness cannot be successful without the repentance, courage, sacrifice, and the other graces of the spirit which are

188

the very heart of religion. In the personal exercise of religious devotion and in the appreciation of great ethical and religious souls like Jesus of Nazareth the individual obtains the best incentives to moral excellence. An educational program which neglects these inspirational phases of the total human experience is fair neither to the potentialities of the private self nor to the possibilities of a better social order.

In the second place, religion can help us cultivate the honest sympathy for our fellows which a time of crisis and trouble always demands. The human race needs comforters; it needs men and women who can inspire in their distressed fellow beings emotional poise and confidence. In religion, love and peace become dominating influences. Through religious insight we discover that our universe is a personal cosmos with a heart that is merciful and kind. Liking to feel that he is acting in conformity with basic laws, man is always encouraged by the faith that the brutality of nature is not the ultimate principle of nature. In friendship and brotherhood we get below the superficial feelings of man. As fundamental sentiments of the race, they are indifferent to danger and depression. One of the great contributions of religion is its abiding confidence in the worth and triumph of sympathy and good will. Whatever one may think of the church and its organizational aims, the historic purpose of the church to establish a kingdom of heaven on earth shines out as one of man's most glorious ideals.

In the third place, in religious experience we have the assurance of a cosmic wisdom and support without

189

which all our human gropings for justice and happiness would lose their basis and meaning. The faith of religion is the dynamic belief that goodness and truth will win. One of my students once answered the direction *Discuss the life and work of Socrates* in this way: " I do not remember anything about Socrates, except that he said that no harm can come to a good man." This belief in the final victory of righteousness is a central theme of Judaism, Platonism, Stoicism, Scholasticism, Christian Science, and Protestantism. Philosophers who have most stressed individual responsibility and freedom, such as Paul, Augustine, Aquinas, Calvin, Kant, and Royce, have emphasized the cosmic foundations of moral law. To most people this belief in the supremacy and power of ethical values is a phase of a larger faith in God; but humanists and naturalists, who do not accept theism, also believe religiously that the forces of social good will be more effective in the long run than the forces of evil. Morale in any social group is a reflection of confidence on the part of the members in the right and power of their cause. Liberal education for democracy must cultivate the religious basis of morale if democracy is to sustain the popular enthusiasm necessary for its survival.

With every allowance for the importance of great ideals of faith in religion, the educated man will insist that beliefs be consistent with reason. He will urge that religionists maintain a faith in the power of the intelligence to solve the perplexing problems of modern civilized life. The standard of reason in

190

religious thinking opposes the uncritical enthusiasm with which some supernaturalists receive the mystical pronouncements of recent science. The rational student will be fully acquainted with the unpredictable contractions and expansions of the astronomical universe, the indeterminacies of the electronic physics, the emergents of creative evolution, and the illogical impulses of dynamic psychology. He will even admit that these irrationalities indicate a spontaneous and creative character in nature. But he will remember that no important contemporary scientist has forsaken the objective methods of observation for any kind of unscientific mysticism. The present widespread retreat of religion from reason must not degenerate into an escape philosophy for timid souls. The beliefs of religion do bring comfort and consolation; but if they are not consistent with the facts and needs of life, they will be deceptive and dangerous. The liberally educated person must make sure that his spiritual idealism is not wishful thinking or emotional indulgence but a thoughtful interpretation of the freedom and value actually present in the world of materialism, machinery, and mammon. The college youth will seek to appreciate the significance of mystical religion for motivation in social reconstruction; but he will not forget that the best methods for improving society must be true to the situations in which man daily lives and to the criteria of strict scientific logic. The race tragically needs human beings inspired with hope and optimism, but it more desperately needs those who can see life steadily, completely, and honestly. The great philosopher Immanuel Kant was fundamentally right in his insight that only ideals which emerge from reason are either worthy enough or powerful enough to move the moral will.

34. *The Understanding Mind*

The fourth characteristic of complete selfhood is *comprehensive understanding.* This feature is the most inclusive and significant of all the aspects of personality discussed in this book. It embraces all the cultural values which are to be found in the perspective of a liberally educated man or woman. It is college life and purpose individualized in the outlook of a single self. To portray the scope of understanding is to enumerate the supreme aims of a liberally educated man. Needless to say, the same ideals apply in the outlook of a woman with a liberal education. I submit ten objectives as the life ideals of an educated man.

1

The educated man will be a fearless, logical, and constructive thinker; and he will be able to express his thoughts in correct, definite, and interesting language.

2

The educated man will know the rules of effective biological and psychological behavior; and, in the light of this knowledge, he will follow the best practices of mental and physical health.

192

3

The educated man will select his lifework on the basis of the most authoritative information in the field of vocational guidance; and he will cultivate the idealistic and altruistic outlook which will prevent his professional career from becoming purely a selfish enterprise.

4

The educated man will be able to appreciate intelligently the contributions of the human spirit in the realms of art, literature, music, and drama; and in arriving at this cultural understanding he will come to know some of the great souls of the race.

5

The educated man, through an intelligent concern for historical studies, will have some appreciation of the major economic, political, and religious forces which have determined the evolution of modern civilized society.

6

The educated man will maintain a lively interest in current events; but he will earnestly strive for an unprejudiced and critical view of the various social forces which are reshaping contemporary institutional life.

7

The educated man, through the attainment of a definite knowledge of the main concepts of the physical and biological sciences, will achieve some appreciative understanding of the natural order and of man's place within it.

THE ART OF SELF-DENIAL

8

The educated man will be aware of the personal responsibility and the social necessity of championing the causes which support, and of destroying the forces which inhibit, the constructive development of the family, the state, the church, and the international order.

9

The educated man will follow the lead of speculative insight to reach a fundamental, comprehensive, reasonable, and harmonious world view, or philosophy.

10

The educated man, through intelligent and reverential devotion to prayer, worship, and the other exercises of the spiritual life, will cultivate a religious experience which will give his life — and that of nature, society, and God — meaning, glory, and value.

If we wish to find a scheme of living in which the above ideals seemed to function in the development of a people, we may well study the mind of ancient Greece. In the great age of Greece we discover the cultural basis of Western civilization. From the standpoint of educational ideals, the Hellenic community of old truly stood foursquare. Its *four walls* became the bulwarks of an abiding intellectual stronghold. The main essentials of any adequate cultural vision were clearly apprehended by the Greeks. What were these four great intellectual objectives of the ancient Hellene? *Science, morality, art,* and *religion.*

194

Democritus, with his quantitative theories of atomism and mechanism, laid the foundations of modern mathematical and technological science. He taught man the intelligibility and controllability of physical nature. Not long afterward came the prince of all who know, Aristotle, who carried the temper and method of science into the realms of biological and sociological evolution.

In the laying of the second wall, morality, Socrates, with his critical interest in the foundations of political excellence, disclosed the claims of intelligent and courageous virtue. The great ethical insights of both the Epicureans and the Stoics found their inspiration in the moral and psychological doctrines of the Sage of Athens. In this Athenian martyr, mankind has found one of its noblest champions of the free and rational conscience.

And when we consider the third great wall of the Greek cultural community, — namely, aesthetics,— Plato, with his clear insight into the resplendent patterns of heaven, shows us how to bring down to earthly human beings the eternal glories of beauty and order. This illustrious son of Apollo forever made artistic and romantic idealism sane and respectable.

Plotinus, who, with his mystical comprehension of cosmic destiny, established the fourth side of the Greek cultural state by substantiating for religion the wonder and efficacy of God, gave, along with Plato and the early Church Fathers, the spiritual experiences of Christianity a philosophical basis and a moral efficacy.

195

The discoveries of these ancient philosophers were extended as later thinkers (like Aquinas, Descartes, Spinoza, Locke, Kant, Hegel, Spencer, James, and Royce) attained new and better knowledge; but the insight of the Greeks into the rationality of nature, the nobility of righteousness, the eternal validity of truth and beauty, and the reality and immanence of God will remain a challenge to seekers after wisdom for ages to come.

The spirit and aims of the cultural tradition, as they have been exemplified in the history of western Europe, are concentrated in the life and purpose of one institution — *the college of liberal arts*. The college is the supreme guardian and disseminator of the aspirations and achievements of the human spirit. As long as mankind is interested in truth, goodness, and beauty, liberal education will survive; and as long as young men and young women wish to learn how to live with courage and wisdom, there will be students in college halls. To institutions of higher learning, mankind is now looking for light and leading. To be a thoughtful undergraduate in these days is a momentous privilege: it is, in a very true sense, to participate in the fight for civilization and freedom. In an abiding belief in *freedom*, *intelligence*, and *morality* our nation will find its soul. In bringing to the hearts and minds of youth this threefold faith the colleges of America will maintain their glory and their power.

196

INDEX

197

199

INDEX